APPROACHING THE CROSS

John's Gospel Witness to Jesus Dying and Rising

Robert A. Gillies

Jenni,

With every blessing

+ Bob Gillies

Epiphany 2018

British Library Cataloguing in Publication Data:
a catalogue record for this publication
is available from the British Library

ISBN   978-1-912052-41-7

Typeset in 11.5pt Minion Pro at Haddington, Scotland

Printing and cover design by
West Port Print and Design, St Andrews

Published with assistance from
the Drummond Trust,
3 Pitt Terrace, Stirling

CONTENTS

Introduction   1

Chapter One   Palm Sunday
                  - Jesus' entry into Jerusalem   6

Chapter Two   Monday in Holy Week
                  – At the home of Lazarus   13

Chapter Three   Tuesday in Holy Week
                  – Sacrifice, suffering and salvation   26

Chapter Four   Wednesday in Holy Week
                  – Trying to understand Judas Iscariot   37

Chapter Five   Maundy Thursday
                  – Jesus' final meal with his disciples   46

Chapter Six   Good Friday
                  – The approach to the cross   57

Chapter Seven   Easter Eve (Holy Saturday)
                  – Jesus is dead   67

Chapter Eight   Easter Sunday
                  – In the garden   79

Bibliography   90

To The Diocese of Aberdeen and Orkney

With affection and gratitude

Introduction

This is a devotional book. It is mainly intended for reading to stimulate thought and reflection in the weeks leading up to and including Easter. Hopefully also it will aid prayer. The theme of the book concerns events that happened to, or around, Jesus in the days that led up to his death. Crucially also I include two chapters, one on his entombment and one on his resurrection. My reference point throughout is the Gospel according to St John and the readings selected from it for various of the services that take place from Palm Sunday to Easter Day. I will return to this in a moment; but first, some background to help set this book in context.

The impetus to write this devotional volume for Lent came to me when a former colleague, Canon John Walker, invited me, on behalf of the churches in the Aberdeenshire town of Inverurie, to deliver five weekday addresses during Holy Week 2016. Extended versions of these addresses comprise Chapters Two to Six below. In preparing them for publication I have added three more to make, as it were, a devotional octave that takes us along the sequence of Jesus arriving in Jerusalem, on what we know as Palm Sunday, to his Easter Sunday resurrection.

The original title for those addresses in Inverurie was 'Approaching the Cross'. Whilst that was surely appropriate enough for Holy Week and the build up to the climax of Good Friday I have thought long and hard about whether or not to keep the same title for this book given that the final chapter concerns Jesus' resurrection, and the penultimate chapter his lying in the tomb.

After much consideration, I have decided to keep the original title. For Holy Saturday (Easter Eve) the shadow of the cross upon which Jesus was killed the day before would have cast long and dark shadows over his followers. Its image would have been difficult to dispel from their minds, as they grieved his loss. The same would be true for those who attended Jesus' grave on that first Easter Sunday. Though they were going to the place of resurrection they did not know that at the time and were only going to Jesus' grave because of what happened on the cross, and because they presumed he would still be dead in his grave. The resurrection of Jesus can only be understood in the light of this and because of the cross of his crucifixion. We cannot say that we live in the light and in the faith of the resurrection if we have not understood what was won for us at so great a cost to Jesus through his dying, death and burial. So, therefore, my original title remains, *Approaching the Cross*.

My subtitle, 'John's Gospel witness to Jesus dying and rising' arises from the decision I have made broadly to follow bible readings from John's Gospel that are provided within the very wide and varied selection of readings recommended for each of these eight days from what is called the church's 'Lectionary'. The Lectionary provides readings for the many varied services that take place on the eight days beginning with Palm Sunday and ending on Easter Sunday.

In each of the four gospels the closing days of Jesus' life are given what seems at first sight to be an entirely disproportionate amount of attention when compared not only to the three years or so of his ministry but also to the remainder of his life which, apart from the birth narratives and childhood accounts in Matthew and Luke, receives no attention at all.

This is particularly so in John's gospel. About a third of the material concerns events in the week when Jesus was executed. I would even go further and say that from Chapter Two of John's gospel onwards, and with the definite advantage of hindsight, one distinctly knows that the events leading up to Jesus' death are being trailed in advance. In many ways this hindsight advantage shapes our perception of those events. However, at a number of points in the chapters below I will be asking you, the reader, to try and imagine what it might be like *not* to know the outcome, even though we do.

A very active and creative New Testament scholar, Richard Burridge, has written extensively and very persuasively in this area. In his *What are the Gospels?*[1] he notes how ancient biographies might well commit significant space to events and circumstances that closely precede the death of their subject. The four gospels give evidence of this fact in their

---

1   Richard A. Burridge, *What are the Gospels? A Comparison with Graeco-Roman Biography,* Cambridge University Press, Cambridge 1992.

account of Jesus' days in Jerusalem prior to his arrest, summary trial and execution.

However, more than this can be said. For, given that our subject is Jesus, we need not be surprised to find that following his death, and not least in John, what took place between his resurrection, his rising from death, and his subsequent ascension into heaven, understood as a period of forty days, also receives significantly considered narrative and teaching space in the gospels.

For the purposes of this book as a devotional work for Lent I have chosen to limit my focus to those eight days that begin with the day we know as Palm Sunday and end with Easter Sunday itself.

Each chapter below begins with the words of a 'Collect', a prayer appropriate to the theme of what follows. I then give the full text of the biblical passage on which I shall focus. The remainder of the chapter is what is called an 'expository reflection' on that scriptural text relevant to that day from the given reading from John's gospel. By sticking close to the biblical text my aim is to offer some thoughts which I pray will, in turn, come close to you as your faith is broadened and deepened as you walk, through these pages, with Jesus to the cross and beyond.

I acknowledge with gratitude those whose assistance and patient consideration has helped this little book become what you now have in your hands. It is all the richer for their improving comment. In particular I must mention those who have read early drafts and provided invaluable comment: Dr Alistair Mason, The Revd Prof David Jasper and Dr Alison Jasper. Residual deficiencies remain, as they must, at my door.

All books such as this begin from a particular personal standpoint and each author has his or her own autobiography that is unique. Since 1977 I have been in holy orders, variously as a deacon, priest and bishop. I was in seminary for five years and before that a technician in a pathology laboratory for four years having left school at sixteen. My upbringing as an only child, principally by my mother and grandparents, due to the poor relationship I had with my father, was in a significantly isolated part of rural north-east Lincolnshire. Reflecting on those times I can recognise that these early years of my life were similarly isolated.

When I started work in the laboratory I struggled with the world of work, with the demands of people around me, and the professional and at times perplexing tasks being required of an adolescent teenager, and only child, straight out of school. What I did at the laboratory and the responsibilities I held are nowadays part of a graduate profession with immature youths of today mercifully spared what I went through. Happily, things did improve for me and for those around me as my four years progressed towards successful Higher National Certificate qualification in Histopathology and Cytology.

I first 'went' to church (the local, sparsely attended, parish church) when I was six weeks old and have been attending church ever since. Unlike many people I have never known atheism.

My marriage to Liz has been and remains a joy and from it we have three wonderful sons. But there has been tragedy. Not least when, towards the end of a Sunday School Christmas party in 1981, I found our then second son, Jonathan, dead in his pram at fifteen weeks of age. Previously, in my pathology career, I had encountered sudden infant death syndrome, 'cot death'. Now I knew it personally. The church where I was working at the time (Christ Church, Edinburgh) lived true Christian support for Liz and I and Patrick our eldest son. For that we remain truly grateful. In due course Patrick was joined by Andrew and Timothy.

None of this can be separated from what I have written below for, even though I have written for the present moment with an eye for the future, every author composes material that reflects where he or she has come from. My hope is that the patient reader will make due allowance for any viewpoint that I have taken which might aggravate or annoy but which, it might be seen, arises from the make-up that is me. Equally, some of the reflections I offer in the chapters below might be helpfully and creatively illuminated as a result of this simple postage stamp autobiography.

The prayers at the start of each chapter are drawn from the Lectionary and Calendar of the Scottish Episcopal Church and the Bible passages from the *New Revised Standard Version*. I also acknowledge with thanks the permission of the Trustees of the Diocese of Aberdeen and Orkney for their permission to use the Diocesan Crest on the dedication page of this book.

In closing I must also thank Canon John Walker for his invitation to give the holy week addresses in Inverurie in 2016 and which spurred me to write this book. The presence of between sixty to ninety folks who gathered for worship each evening that week and heard what I had to say was a great encouragement and humbling experience. I also thank those of 'Inverurie Churches Together' who prepared and led ecumenical worship on those occasions when five of the addresses below, albeit in abbreviated form, were first given.

Robert A. Gillies
Ash Wednesday 2018

Chapter One
PALM SUNDAY
Jesus' entry into Jerusalem

A Prayer
Assist us mercifully with your help,
Lord God of our salvation,
that we may enter with joy
into the celebration of those mighty acts
whereby you give us life and immortality;
through Jesus Christ our Lord.
Amen

John 12:12-16
Jesus' Triumphal Entry into Jerusalem
[12]The next day the great crowd that had come to the festival heard that Jesus was coming to Jerusalem. [13]So they took branches of palm trees and went out to meet him, shouting,
"Hosanna! Blessed is the one who comes in the name of the Lord – the King of Israel!"
[14]Jesus found a young donkey and sat on it; as it is written:
[15]"Do not be afraid, daughter of Zion.
Look, your king is coming,
sitting on a donkey's colt!"
[16]His disciples did not understand these things at first; but when Jesus was glorified, then they remembered that these things had been written of him and had been done to him.[1]

---

1 Alternative reading set for the Liturgy of the Palms, Year B.

Introduction

We begin this sequence of eight reflections as Jesus arrives at the edge of Jerusalem. As we shall see in Chapter Two he has already been to the home of Mary, Martha and Lazarus. Now Jesus must enter Jerusalem and meet the fate that will, with inevitably increasing drama, unfold before him.

The Setting

Jesus has left the home of Mary, Martha and Lazarus in Bethany. The journey from Bethany to Jerusalem is not far; perhaps about seven miles. Many people had gathered at the house in Bethany to see Jesus as the news of Lazarus being made alive, and emerging from his grave, after being presumed dead for four days, had spread quickly. It was at the command of Jesus that Lazarus walked out of his grave. It is therefore unsurprising that many were both curious and fascinated. As a result, they wanted to see Jesus. Many came to the house expressly for this purpose.

Little wonder therefore that many also gathered and greeted him as he arrived in Jerusalem. The Feast of Passover was approaching and the local population was already massively swollen by those attending from far and wide. Jesus' reputation had gone before him. He was, you might say, an extra 'attraction' for them to come and see. They could not know then what would be happening to him over the next few days. Still less would they even begin to conjecture what was to be found to have happened that first Easter Sunday morning, exactly a week later.

Let us now look a little more closely at what happened as Jesus arrived on the outskirts of Jerusalem.

The Triumphal Welcome

In the passage from John's gospel at the start of this chapter it would seem, as we have just noted, that from amongst the huge numbers of people gathered in Jerusalem for Passover "a great crowd" welcomed him on his approach to the city. The crowd did so, seemingly waving branches from palm trees accompanied by shouts of 'hosanna' in a manner not unlike the welcome given other leaders in the past.[1] The perception we have of this crowd greeting an incoming king is no coincidence. At the human level of their understanding they fully believed that this is what they were doing.

The song on their lips, "Blessed is the one that comes in the name of the Lord" is Psalm 118 (at verse 26, the only occasion in John's gospel when the verb 'blessed' is used). This is a psalm of thanksgiving for deliverance from enemies. It is Jesus who, in the eyes of the crowd, is to be the perceived victorious conqueror, will bring this about. The shouts of the people, with the familiar acclamation, 'Hosanna' echoes the welcome to a king.

So, whilst the people considered Jesus as Lord very much in terms of a saving messiah who, politically, would lead them into freedom as a people and as a nation, others, not least Jesus himself along with the author of John's gospel, considered his Lordship very differently. At a technical level I can explain this. As God, enfleshed in human form, Jesus' Lordship is entirely derived from his oneness with God the Father, whose voice and actions Jesus lived. The Lordship of Jesus was supremely that of the leader who *serves* and who, as we shall see as these reflections proceed through the days of Holy Week, *embodied that service in humility*.

Mayer[2] makes the interesting figurative point that the day upon which Jesus entered Jerusalem was also the day when the lambs that were to be sacrificed for the Passover Festival were selected. Here Jesus, known throughout Christian history as the Lamb of God, for he too went to be slaughtered at the time of Passover, makes his own entry into that city where his life would be extinguished and his blood poured out because of human sinfulness.

Ironically, and within a few days, the crowd in Jerusalem assembled before Pilate at Jesus' summary trial were to shout that they had "no king but Caesar."[3] A crowd welcomed Jesus into Jerusalem as their saviour. He would win victory for them and remove Roman domination, they foresaw.

---

1 Richard Burridge (*John*, BRF, Abingdon 2008) notes on page 154 that whilst the words for 'palm' and 'branches' are rare they nonetheless are found in the "accounts of greeting the successful Maccabean leaders" as given in 2 Maccabees 10:7 and also in 1 Maccabees 13:51. I am grateful to Alistair Mason, one of my critical readers, for reminding me that ". . . in Maccabees [the context is] . . . God's honour, not . . . greeting a king."

2 See *New International Dictionary of New Testament Theology*, vol. 1, ed. Colin Brown, 628.

3 John 19:15.

However, and just a few days later, the crowd in Jerusalem would be baying for his blood.

Jesus' Humble Response

Jesus, no doubt still with shouts of acclamation and swaying palm branches before him, takes a donkey colt and rides on it into the city. This would have been an incongruous sight. No saving conqueror should so abase himself, some in the crowd might have been murmuring. And yet, this is what Jesus did. Perhaps he was, even at this stage, trying yet again to disabuse those around him of a flawed understanding of the kingly leadership and victory that was to be his.

All four gospels report Jesus riding into Jerusalem on the colt of a donkey; though young the animal would have been deemed old enough for the task. Travel on such beasts would have been common, particularly amongst the merchant classes or those with cash enough to afford such an animal, and would not have occasioned any thought that they were behaving below their station in life.

However, for someone just minutes before acclaimed and welcomed as a liberating king, riding into the city he was to free on a donkey was unconscionable. At the very least a substantial horse would be the expected mount. Perhaps at the sight of this first self-abasement by Jesus some in the triumphalist crowd of greeting might have discreetly melted away both for fear of shame and also because of the incongruity between their expectation of Jesus and what they now saw him doing.

John, recounting these events in his gospel, uses words familiar to him from the Hebrew scriptures (in broad terms what we now have as the Old Testament) to depict what happens. He is drawing from something that is already familiar and well known to narrate, and in part to explain something similar, foreshadowed long ago, taking place 'now', as it were:

> Rejoice greatly, O daughter Zion!
> Shout aloud, O daughter Jerusalem!
> Lo, your king comes to you;
> triumphant and victorious is he,
> humble and riding on a donkey,
> on a colt, the foal of a donkey.[4]

---

4 Zechariah 9:9.

Crucially we note that in the account from John's gospel the opening words, taken here from Zechariah 9:9, "Rejoice greatly . . ." are replaced with "Fear not . . ." Yet again John is trying to show how Jesus' leadership into victory is different both in kind and in content from that of any human messianic figure. Writing after the resurrection the author of John's gospel would have been able to see what others immediately surrounding those events could not see. Namely that Jesus is a messianic, priestly, figure.[5] He is fulfilling prophecy of old and dutifully living his obedience to the will of God fully. He is not mounting a political campaign.

This is noted in John 12:16 when the gospel writer says of the disciples that, ". . . [they] did not understand these things at first; but when Jesus was glorified, then they remembered that these things had been written of him and had been done to him." Their failure to understand Jesus' teaching and instruction was most evident in what he forecast to them that he would be humiliated, would suffer and would die. In other words, for the disciples, the 'penny had yet to drop'. By way of aside we note that this is the context in which Judas Iscariot would be led to betray Jesus. The disciples didn't know the outcome of the tumultuous events that are beginning to unfold. Dismay was to enfold them all entirely. Little wonder, perhaps, that one of them at least, would be led to desperate measures. I will return to this theme in Chapter Four below.

My own conjecture reflects the view expressed by Ruth Edwards in her book on John's Gospel.[6] Even though the disciples had previously put their faith in Jesus they seem to have little awareness of what the implications of this might mean, let alone understanding the significance of all that Jesus had taught them through his words and work. So, on this point, if the disciples did not understand the meaning of what Jesus was saying and doing then neither would the crowd. Upon the issues, set out before us here, we must remain open and allow our minds to wonder what Jesus' entry into Jerusalem might have looked like, and to give our imagination full and free expression to conjure in our mind's eye any number of possible options by which the events unfolded. So then, what might have happened?

Jesus' entry into Jerusalem – what might it have looked like?

---

5 Ruth Edwards notes on this are informative. See her *Discovering John,* SPCK, London 2014, 78.

6 Ruth Edwards, *op. cit.*, 116.

We are not told in John's Gospel whether the crowd followed Jesus into Jerusalem as he rode in on the young donkey, though the other three gospels seem to indicate that at least that was how his journey into the city began. Matthew, in his gospel, is particularly clear that this was how Jesus did enter Jerusalem. But we are not told in John whether, if the crowd did accompany Jesus' entry to the city, they did so with palm branches waving, and 'hosannas' ringing out, even though from Matthew, with Mark and Luke, we might well imagine that they did.

If it was the case that some deserted Jesus at the city limits perhaps they chose to do so because they did not want to be associated with a man they had presumed to be a king, but who had then abased himself in their presence by riding on a donkey. If the arrival of Jesus in Jerusalem did not arouse the huge clamour that Matthew's gospel suggests was the case, "with the whole city in turmoil asking [about Jesus], 'Who is this?'" then that could explain why there was no intervention by any of the governing authorities, especially the Roman army. For them to have intervened they would have needed significant notice of Jesus' approach to the city for them to be diverted from their more likely focus, the Temple Mount. They would also need to have been forewarned as to the significance of Jesus as someone more deliberately in need of their attention over against most or all of the other individual males thronging into Jerusalem and swelling the already vast crowd present in the city.

That the Roman soldiers would be alert to trouble rising at the time of Passover is attested by Josephus:[7]

> When the festival called Passover was at hand at which it is our custom to serve unleavened bread, a large multitude from all quarters assembled for it. [Cumanus] fearing that their presence might afford occasion for an uprising, ordered one company of soldiers to take up arms and stand guard on the porticoes of the temple so as to quell any uprising that might occur. This had been in fact the usual practice of previous procurators of Judaea at the festivals.

It is likely that the Temple's own safeguarding authorities would be aware of Jesus and of his potential nuisance value. But if they had not been forewarned that he was entering the city they too would not have noticed one traveller being welcomed any more than any other of the travellers perhaps being similarly greeted.

---

7 Josephus, *Jewish Antiquities XX,* para 106.

Even if the welcome given to Jesus with singing and palm branches waving was a wide-scale event and even if it lasted a long time (and we are not told how long it lasted) we must take it that it caused no obvious disturbance such as might have concerned the respective law enforcement authorities for them to initiate immediate intervention. Amidst all the rest of the hullabaloo going on at the time Jesus' arrival might not have been noticeable much beyond the ensemble who were part of it.

To all of this we may add the further note that in John's Gospel Jesus is presented as a frequent visitor to Jerusalem from Galilee. If so, why then should the Temple police think anything was different about this particular arrival as against any of Jesus' other visits to the city? In such a crowd at a major gathering, then as now, there would be any admixture of mendicant troublemakers, annoying peddlers, upstarts thinking more of themselves than they deserved, as well as attention-seeking preachers and so much more. Against this backcloth, perhaps to the Roman soldiers with an Empire to defend against potentially serious insurgencies and rebellion, Jesus did not stand out with any great significance at this stage in the week. No army followed him and for all intents and purposes he and his followers carried no significant weaponry.

In respect of Jesus' profile before the authorities, both in the Temple and with the Roman guard, things were soon to change.

Postscript

As we now come to the end of this reflection and turn to Chapter Two so we find before us a reading from John's gospel that takes us back to events that had occurred before Jesus' triumphal entry into Jerusalem. It is a function of the readings set from John's gospel by the lectionary of daily readings that we have this ebb and flow, this to and fro, of events that lead us up to the death of Jesus.

Chapter Two
MONDAY IN HOLY WEEK
At the home of Lazarus

A Prayer

Almighty God,
whose most dear Son went not up to joy, but first he suffered pain,
and entered not into his glory before he was crucified:
mercifully grant, that we, walking in the way of his cross,
may find it none other than the way of life and peace;
through the same Jesus Christ our Lord, who lives and reigns with
you, in the unity of the Holy Spirit, one God, world without end.
Amen

John 12:1-11
Mary Anoints Jesus

Six days before the Passover, Jesus came to Bethany, where Lazarus
was, whom Jesus had raised from the dead. ²There they made him a
supper; Martha served, and Lazarus was one of those at table with
him. ³Mary took a pound of costly ointment of pure nard and anointed
the feet of Jesus and wiped his feet with her hair; and the house was
filled with the fragrance of the ointment. ⁴But Judas Iscariot, one of his
disciples (he who was to betray him), said, ⁵"Why was this ointment
not sold for three hundred denarii and given to the poor?" ⁶This he
said, not that he cared for the poor but because he was a thief, and as
he had the money box he used to take what was put into it. ⁷Jesus said,
"Let her alone, let her keep it for the day of my burial. ⁸The poor you
always have with you, but you do not always have me."

The Plot to Kill Lazarus

⁹When the great crowd of the Jews learned that he was there, they
came, not only on account of Jesus but also to see Lazarus, whom
he had raised from the dead. ¹⁰So the chief priests planned to put
Lazarus also to death, ¹¹because on account of him many of the Jews
were going away and believing in Jesus.[1]

---

1 Reading set for Daily Eucharist, Year C.

Introduction

In Chapter One my reflection turned around Jesus arriving in Jerusalem on a donkey, part of one of the set readings for Palm Sunday at the start of Holy Week. Now finding ourselves on the Monday of Holy Week as we trace the lectionary bible readings set for us to use, it is interesting to discover that, amongst these, the given passage from John's Gospel takes a step back in time prior to the arrival of Jesus in Jerusalem, by a day or so in fact, to the arrival of Jesus at the home of Lazarus in the village of Bethany. From Bethany it would then be little more than a few hours walk onwards to Jerusalem.

The setting

So then, we read that Jesus has arrived at the home of Lazarus. The time is approaching Passover, it is six days away. A meal is being prepared for Jesus. Martha and Mary are key figures with Lazarus at this meal. Our thoughts in this chapter will centre around what took place at that meal.

First of all, we note that we can't be exactly sure when the actual meal itself took place though it was most likely to be the evening of what we would know as the Saturday before Good Friday. In those days evening was recognised as the start of the day to follow. That was when the day began. Accordingly, a meal was taken with a night's sleep to follow before setting out to do that which needed to be accomplished during the daylight hours.

Clearly Lazarus, Martha and Mary each knew Jesus. In the previous chapter of John's Gospel the two women had spoken with Jesus in familiar tones and faithful terms when he went to the place where Lazarus had earlier lain dead. Lazarus had been dead for four days. It was a timespan beyond that which mourners, in their cultural context, would have been expected to visit the grave and was beyond the three days when, it was then understood, that the 'spirit' of a person remained with a corpse before departing. Lazarus therefore had been very dead. And yet, John's Gospel recounts that in Jesus' presence and at Jesus' command, Lazarus had come out of his grave alive.

Anticipations and echoes

There is no surprise, however, that Jesus, Martha, Mary and Lazarus (with disciples) were together at a meal. They knew each other and sitting down for a meal is what they would have been expected to do together. And yet in this case their gathering prefigured other things.

First, Lazarus had emerged from his grave, alive after being dead, still wrapped in his linen grave clothes. A week later, or thereabouts, given the timescale of the events as recorded in John's Gospel, Jesus was to rise from his tomb, albeit in his case freed of all earthly encumbrances and wrappings.

Second, the meal at the home of Lazarus, with Mary and Martha, also anticipated, or perhaps better, prefigured, the last supper Jesus was to have with his disciples some six or so days later. At that later meal, Jesus washed the feet of his disciples with water. By contrast, here, in the home of Lazarus, Lazarus' sister, Mary, anointed Jesus' feet with what would have been hugely expensive spices. In both cases the action undertaken, the former by Mary, the latter by Jesus, would have been something recognised as humble service, even to the point of being embarrassingly and self-humiliatingly servile.

Next, the spice Mary used for the anointing of Jesus is 'nard'. This is a fragrant oil extracted from the root of the spikenard plant, *Nardostachys jatamansi*, a flowering plant of the Valerian family. It grows in the wild in the Himalayas of Nepal, China, and India. Mary used all she had in the jar. A year's worth of salary. The stuff would have been very expensive to buy, not least because of the distance it would have had to have been brought from source, and thus would have been available only to those with cash to spend on items of such luxury.

If, on this surmising, the household was financially well-off, the actions of Mary in kneeling down at Jesus' feet, in the posture of a servant and slave, would have seemed even more socially offensive than her extravagant fragrant application of this unction upon one for whom her devotion was more than self-evident. There is however much more than this to challenge any onlookers. By speaking to her, or rather to the others about her in the way he did, Jesus courted significant disapproval. Moreover, by accepting what would seem to any onlookers to be an immoral and offensive level of affection between people who were not related, Jesus had cast aside norms and social conventions commonplace at the time.

Scarcely is the significance of this commented on by many, unless from a feminist perspective. In situations such as this Jesus advanced the cause of female emancipation by what he did here as well as by what he did in those other situations not unlike it where he broke the taboos of his day. For a woman to be seen in public without a veil, or to speak to men outside of one's doors as he did elsewhere, were forbidden. What happens in this passage is but one example of what Langley calls Jesus' "flagrant flouting of convention" and thus is "indicative of his sense of justice and equality".[2]

The anointing

Just about all commentators on this passage recognise that whilst Mary's action could be seen as an anointing of a king it is more likely, given the context, to be an anointing in preparation for death. In this sense, this action further anticipates and prefigures what Joseph of Arimathea did when he petitioned for the body of Jesus (see John 19:38ff and Chapter Seven below) and who, with Nicodemus, anointed it in death. This much Jesus seemed to recognise in his rejoinder to Judas Iscariot, when Judas considered that the spice could have been sold with the proceeds going to alleviate the needs of the poor. Jesus' challenge to Judas was that Mary had anointed him with oil reserved by her, and presumably the family, for the day of his burial.

Jesus, simply to clarify, isn't speaking literally here. His death is still several days away. Rather, he is using a figure of speech to heighten tension in the narrative by means of the simple rhetorical device of referring to the death which was coming to him *as though* it were that day. It is worth remembering that the writers who put the gospels together in the written form that we now have them did so knowing, as we do, the outcome of the story. Because the outcome is crucial for the Christian narrative there is little wonder the writer of this passage wove through his account hints, suggestions and signs of what was to come as the gospel pages turn.

Let us not forget also that reclining at the table alongside or near to Jesus at the meal is the resuscitated Lazarus – a man no longer dead.[3] Lazarus is the one who has already laid in a grave. Jesus, with this anointing, is being prepared to enter his. As these friends gathered, Jesus had already demonstrated his mastery over death by returning the dead brother Lazarus to his sisters. His own mastery through resurrection was still to come. We shall return to this in due course.

---

2 M. Langley, 'War' in *The New International Dictionary of New Testament Theology*, vol. 3, 980.

3 In my *Three Days in Holy Week*, Handsel Press, Edinburgh, 9, I describe the posture of those at a meal at the time of Jesus.

In the gospel that bears his name, Mark concludes his story of the anointing (14:6-9) with the words, "Truly I tell you, wherever the good news is proclaimed in the whole world, what she has done will be told in remembrance of her." This context is indicative of something further. To explain what I mean by this we recall that at the last supper of Jesus with his disciples he blessed bread and wine. The ancient tradition begun then and continued today echoes Mark's comment on Mary's actions, namely that Jesus' followers should "do this in remembrance of [him]". (1 Corinthians 11:23-26)

If this is so then the links between the meal at the home of Lazarus and Mary's anointing of Jesus with washing of the disciples' feet at the Passover meal with his disciples become evocatively powerful. The connection between the actions of mutual service in humility and the remembrance (the remembering) of them as a stimulus for us doing the same here and now is unavoidably real for Christian life and practice. The development of the eucharistic, the holy communion, tradition of the church is inseparable from these biblical antecedents where, on each occasion, friends gathered together to share a meal and something dramatic happened.

Simply for the record we note there are differences of detail between John and Mark's account of this meal at Bethany and in what took place there. In Mark, for example, Mary anoints Jesus' head. But it seems to me, as it does to most commentators, that the same incident is being recounted. Matthew's account is similar to that of Mark. The Gospel writers saw no need to iron out differences between their texts. The overall truth of their accounts would always take precedence over forensic detail minutiae.

We must now move on to Judas' protest at Mary's extravagance.

Judas protested

Judas, it seems, was the money-holder for Jesus and the group of disciples. The "common purse" (John 12:6) that he kept the money in might more accurately be described as a money-box. The word used for this is *glossokomon* and has linguistic provenance in classical Greek from the 2nd century BC to the 2nd AD. In the New Testament it occurs only twice, both here and in John 13:29 where it also refers to Judas' holding the common purse.

Violation of the Eighth Commandment, "Thou shalt not steal" would be a significant offence, not just in relation to any civil law at the time but rather because it broke a divine commandment and thus was contrary to God's will. For a group such as the disciples, theft of the money that was held in common would be a breach of human trust. As a result, the seeds of murmuring disquiet would be sown within the group.

However, there is another side to the story. It is important to note that Judas cited concern for the poor as his objection to Mary's lavish treatment of Jesus in her anointing of him with such richly perfumed and hugely expensive unguent. In this regard, perhaps, we might have some sympathy with his concern. Here's a personal story.

In recent times I have had experience of three senior church officials travelling, quite literally, half way round the world to see me. Their intention was to explain something to me which, in my view, could have just as easily been done by email. But such was their need to explain a situation and to give me a personal apology for something they'd misjudged, that they felt they had to do this in person. Their actions betokened a level of carefulness and personal attention that, again in their view, justified the expense of the three of them taking air fares for what was a relatively short visit. They hired a local translator to join them as well.

I recognise their charity and thoughtfulness. But I remain unconvinced that the expense was justified as I was in no way in need of any personal apology from them. In this instance, and quoting Judas with agreement, the money that paid for those airfares "could have been given to the poor"!

This is where I feel Judas is closer to us than has been allowed in the history of the church. Take the Oberammergau Passion Play for example.

For most of its history all the way from its inception in 1634 as a thank-offering to God for protecting the village from the ravages of the plague, the text of the Oberammergau Passion Play has been notoriously anti-Semitic. The 1934 production, seen by Hitler, was lauded by him. It offered, so official Third Reich propaganda declared, "peasant drama . . . inspired by the consecrating power of the soil". Effort which, providentially, did not succeed, was even made to bring the then text even more fully into line with official Nazi ideology.

Since the Second World War, redactions of the text, and its on-stage portrayals, have thankfully lessened the play's previously overt anti-Semitism and sought to go a considerable way towards portraying the passion of Christ as a drama in the political and religious interplay between a Gentile Roman occupying force and the religious living history of Jews in confrontation with Jesus.

By way of interesting anecdote, when I delivered the shortened version of this Chapter at Inverurie in Aberdeenshire in 2016 I was approached by a member of that audience afterwards who told me that, when he lived briefly in Oberammergau, at the 1970 Passion Play he saw the man who played Judas Iscariot walking home from rehearsal one occasion. He was still wearing the bright yellow costume allotted to him, and which thus made him very distinctive. He was 'hissed at' in the street. This was not a continuation of theatre. This was for real. Such disturbing insult and verbal assault, when personally directed, is deeply worrying irrespective of whether they considered Judas Iscariot (and the man who portrayed him on stage) as an archetypal traitor or archetypal Jew. I will reflect on Judas Iscariot again in Chapter Four.[4]

Anti-Semitism is a sad factor in European cultural and religious history as well as a current frightening reality. And it needn't surprise us to find that some of its roots are there in the Biblical narrative itself. The passage we are looking at here deliberately put Judas Iscariot, the man trusted with Jesus and the disciples' shared common money, in a bad light.

Somehow I cannot help but feel sadness for Judas Iscariot. Not just for what he was to do by betraying Jesus. But also because Judas stood up for the needs of the poor when, before him, he saw what he considered to be needless waste as luxurious nard was poured over Jesus. It might be an instructive exercise for each of us, should ever we criticise Judas Iscariot, to imagine ourselves not gazing with scornful annoyance at some woebegone figure in history but looking directly into a mirror at an all too familiar face that might not have behaved any better than did Judas that evening.

The problem of the poor

In every theological training course, normally within the structure of philosophical theology, the student will encounter what is known as 'the problem of evil' or as it is sometimes more comprehensively titled, 'the problem of good and evil'. Basically the dilemmas that are considered under this heading are those which arise when one asks how a good and loving, and a benevolent and all-powerful God can allow suffering to continue in the world. This issue was once characterised by Boston University professor, Edgar Sheffield Brightman, as a 'dysteleological surd'. Put simply this means the problem won't ever go away no matter how hard you try. It's there to stay.

---

4 With the kind permission of Mr Derek Murray.

It is the same with the poor. Walking down the main street of every UK city you will find the poor sitting wrapped in sleeping bags sometimes seeking to catch your eye, or sometimes past the point of seeking one's attention as, longingly, even if silently, the unavoidable entreaty presents itself, and of which Bing Crosby so tellingly sang, "Brother, can you spare a dime".

> They used to tell me
> I was building a dream—
> And so
> I followed the mob—
> Where there was earth to plough,
> Or guns to bear,
> I was always there—
> Right on the job.
>
> They used to tell me
> I was building a dream—
> With peace
> And glory ahead...
> Why should I be standing in line ...
> Just waiting for bread?
>
> Once I built a railroad,
> Made it run,
> Made it race
> Against time—
> Once I built a railroad,
> Now it's done.
> Brother, can you spare a dime?
>
> Once I built a tower,
> To the sun,
> Brick and rivet and lime ...
> Once I built a tower,
> Now it's done.
> Brother, can you spare a dime?

Once in khaki suits,
Gee, we looked swell—
Full of that
    Yankee Doodle-De-Dum!
Half a million boots
Went sloggin' thru hell—
I was the kid
    With the drum.

Say, don't you remember . . .
They called me Al?
It was Al
    All the time.
Say, don't you remember?
I'm your pal . . .
Buddy, can you spare a dime?[5]

If I am to be honest I am not comfortable walking past the increasing number of people holding forward begging cups or sitting in their sleeping bags next to a little box or cloth cap hoping to receive charity from those mostly passing by. I am even more uncomfortable when I am wearing a dog collar and am one of those who does pass by. "My 'dime' would do nothing for them," I try to convince myself as I walk on. I add, in this internal conversation with my own conscience, "it isn't the right way to help the poor". The issue that haunts me is that I'm not one of the poor. Perhaps I would see things differently if I was sitting where they sit rather than hastening my step onwards in my comfortable shoes. The three hundred denarii that Judas Iscariot felt was so wantonly wasted on Jesus remains, if I may speak in personally applied metaphor, in my case not so much wasted as held on to in my pocket.

"The poor you always have with you" were Jesus' words both to chide Judas as well as to protect Mary; "Leave her alone", Jesus said to Judas, ". . . let her keep it for the day of my burial".[6] One day Jesus would not be around and she would not be able ever again to do what today she then could. It is worth noting that only in this location and similarly in the parallel passages Mark 14:7 and Matthew 26:11 does Jesus place giving of alms to the needy second in priority.

---

5 Lyric by E.Y. 'Yip' Harburg, music by Jay Gorney, from Americana (1932).
6 John 12:7-8 (slightly altered from NRSV).

On this basis Jesus defends the extravagant use of the perfume. We need not view this as a selfish action on his part. Burial rituals were important for the people of his day. After Jesus' death, as recorded in John 19:38ff., Joseph of Arimathea, as we have noted, saw fit to anoint the body of Jesus, thus signifying his devotion to Jesus as well as fulfilling obedience to Jewish Law. Nicodemus provided a substantial amount of aloes and myrrh for this rite, again a very costly volume.

Hemer notes, "The Jews did not embalm like the Egyptians, but myrrh and the other aromatic spices represented the preservation of the body, and this to the Jewish mind was the prerequisite of resurrection."[7] The use of spices in burial rituals was therefore of great importance. In this context Jesus is clearly saying that almsgiving has to take second place to an act of devoted extravagance for someone on the pathway to death.

By way of a personal anecdote on a similar theme I remember vividly a conversation I had once with Belgian friends on the subject of burial rituals. I recounted that the normal practice in most areas of Britain, for the majority of people, was to acquire the cheapest coffin available and not to make any issue of it in any way. When my mother died the funeral director, whom I knew personally, simply showed me three stain finishes (dark, medium and light) to the veneer that would be the outer surface of her chipboard coffin. My Belgian friends were horrified at such seemingly casual and disrespectful 'off-handedness'. Where they came from (both culturally and geographically) great care, they told me, was taken to choose the best coffin that could be afforded. No expense, it seemed to me from what they said, should be spared for such a moment. My attitude remains, I am not ashamed to admit, much more utilitarian and pragmatic.

And what of Lazarus

Thus far Lazarus has not been the centre of the dramatic exchanges between Jesus and Judas, or between Jesus and Mary or Jesus and Martha. So then, what of Lazarus?

The gospel of John in Chapter eleven recounts the story that Lazarus had died, had been buried four days, but that on Jesus' arrival at his grave Lazarus had been revivified. Here he was at the meal table with his sisters and Jesus alive and, for all intents and purposes, well.

---

7 C. J. Hemer in 'Bury' in the *New International Dictionary of New Testament Theology*, vol. 1, 266.

What had happened to Lazarus had, it would seem, become something of a local story. People were coming to find Lazarus to see for themselves that if what they had heard was actually true. When they did it appears that some of them went to tell the Temple authorities whilst others affirmed their faith in Jesus, contrary to the wishes of the Temple's inner circle of leaders. As a consequence, both Jesus and Lazarus were the focus of their disquiet; Jesus because he had raised Lazarus from the dead and Lazarus because he was evidence of the fact, "since it was on account of him that many of the Jews were deserting and were believing in Jesus." (John 12:11) The Chief Priests and Pharisees concerns are succinctly put in the report of their meeting of the 'council', "If we let [Jesus] go on like this, everyone will believe in him, and the Romans will come and destroy both our holy place and our nation." (John 11:47b) In passing we simply note the textual echo from this verse back to 12:11, ". . . it was on account of [Lazarus] that many of the Jews were deserting and believing in Jesus."

In order to give some context to what is being said here it will be useful to look at the way in which the New Testament addresses death. As distinct from its classical portrayal death is not the final end for humankind. In something like seventy-five locations the word *nekros* (meaning 'dead', or 'dead person') is placed in the text as the object of a range of words that refer to resurrection *(anastasis)*, or *egeiro* (to awaken) or similar such. Death, we can see, is being interpreted in the light of the resurrection of Jesus. Coenen,[8] whose work I am drawing from here, also cites other and similar combinations where death is seen in relation to, for example, 'making alive'.

From this biblical and particularly New Testament standpoint a doctrinal theology of death and resurrection arises. In that Jesus is raised from the dead so too death is done away with for others.

In his day, and in the context of this passage, at the command of the human Jesus Lazarus was raised from the dead. In straightforward terms this was given as a sign that Jesus could, and would, overcome the limitations of death. Clearly for Lazarus another day would come when he would have to die. But his death, and all deaths, would now be seen in the light of Jesus' capacity to overcome all death and that as 1 Corinthians 15 puts it death, as a total finality, is done away with in the victory of Jesus over death.

---

8 L. Coenen in 'Death' *In the New International Dictionary of New Testament Theology,* vol. 3, 445f.

Simple (even if puzzling) signs of this happening in ordinary life indicate that an anticipated death need not result that way. In my own pastoral ministry stand three separate incidents where with death as the given or likely outcome for those individuals, it was not to be. I recount two of them in other locations. The third, with permission, is as follows:

In the spring of 2013 someone I know from Dundee was critically, in fact very critically ill at Aberdeen Royal Infirmary. I received a telephone call about 4am from his wife to say that she and her son were travelling from Dundee to see him as they had been advised by the hospital to come as the medical staff thought he was likely to die.

I arrived first, saw him, and then waited in the intensive care unit waiting-room for the wife and son to arrive. We talked when they did and we followed through what we had spoken about on the phone namely that he was *in extremis*, unlikely to live, and that I would anoint him for healing, if not in this life then for the next. Popularly this is known as the last rites.

We went to the bedside. He was attached to a life support machine and monitors. The one that monitors the heart rhythm was showing a line that was flickering and jumping in an erratic fashion demonstrating a severe irregular rhythm. From my medically lay perspective I don't understand these machines, but it was clear that things were not good for him.

Though he was unconscious (I think in a medically induced coma), I told him who was with me, his wife, son, a doctor and two nurses, said what was to happen. I then prayed for him, recited the Lord's Prayer, and anointed him with holy oil with prayer for healing.

The instant I finished the prayer of final commendation and blessing the displays on the monitors steadied; the one that indicated the heart rhythm flat-lined and then showed a shallow but now regular blip as his heart resumed a more normal, if weak, rhythm. The doctor said, "I don't understand that". The nurses looked at each other. And they got on with their medical stuff. He was not, at that time, receiving any infusions or other immediate treatment that would regulate the heart rhythm back to a normal state, or which would otherwise account for what happened.

That narrative will never be reported in any medical journal. It would not stand the test of scientific evidential testimony that its validity be attested by its capacity to be repeatable. Nonetheless, from the perspective of Christian faith and practice, it can stand as testimony of the concurrence of prayer with a sign of God's kingdom becoming real now. Why this should happen for this man and not for others is something I cannot tell. In this testimony there is more enigma than hard evidence.[9]

The wife at least could make the link between prayer and a providential outcome. So could I. Two weeks later when the man emerged from his coma we told him the story. Whilst he had no memory of it he was nonetheless glad to be alive, and as I write this, remains so.[10]

I end this Chapter with reference to Ruth Edwards' *Discovering John*.[11] She speaks of Jesus' 'power to give life' and notes how, "... after healing a lame man, Jesus foretold that the dead would hear the voice of God's Son and live, and that those in the tombs would hear it and come forth."

The story of Lazarus coming from his tomb prefigures Jesus' own rising, and more immediately, sets the scene for his own teaching on the resurrection. From his grave Lazarus emerges still bound with his death-body bandages and returns to his normal life, "... temporarily, for he will die again ..." Jesus, in his rising from death, leaves his wrappings behind and opens a way to eternal life where human death will be no more but henceforth will be that portal through which mortals can pass into an eternity with him.

---

9 I am grateful to Dr Paul Cooper and Dr Julian Chilvers, both Consultant Anaesthetists, for helpful comment on this narrative.
10 This narrative is included with permission.
11 70.

Chapter Three
TUESDAY IN HOLY WEEK
Suffering, sacrifice and salvation

A Prayer
O God,
who by the passion of your blessed Son,
made an instrument of shameful death to be for us the means of life:
grant us so to glory in the cross of Christ,
that we may gladly suffer pain and loss;
for the sake of your Son, our Saviour Jesus Christ,
who lives and reigns with you,
in the unity of the Holy Spirit,
one God, world without end.
Amen

John 12:20-36
Some Greeks Wish to See Jesus
[20]Now among those who went up to worship at the feast were some Greeks. [21]So these came to Philip, who was from Bethsaida in Galilee, and said to him, "Sir, we wish to see Jesus." [22]Philip went and told Andrew; Andrew went with Philip and they told Jesus. [23]And Jesus answered them, "The hour has come for the Son of man to be glorified. [24]Truly, truly, I say to you, unless a grain of wheat falls into the earth and dies, it remains alone; but if it dies, it bears much fruit. [25]He who loves his life loses it, and he who hates his life in this world will keep it for eternal life. [26]If any one serves me, he must follow me; and where I am, there shall my servant be also; if any one serves me, the Father will honour him.

Jesus Speaks about His Death
[27]"Now is my soul troubled. And what shall I say? 'Father, save me from this hour'? No, for this purpose I have come to this hour. [28]Father, glorify thy name." Then a voice came from heaven, "I have glorified it, and I will glorify it again." [29]The crowd standing by heard

it and said that it had thundered. Others said, "An angel has spoken to him." [30]Jesus answered, "This voice has come for your sake, not for mine. [31]Now is the judgment of this world, now shall the ruler of this world be cast out; [32]and I, when I am lifted up from the earth, will draw all men to myself." [33]He said this to show by what death he was to die. [34]The crowd answered him, "We have heard from the law that the Christ remains for ever. How can you say that the Son of man must be lifted up? Who is this Son of man?" [35]Jesus said to them, "The light is with you for a little longer. Walk while you have the light, lest the darkness overtake you; he who walks in the darkness does not know where he goes. [36]While you have the light, believe in the light, that you may become sons of light."[1]

---

1 Reading set for Daily Eucharist, Tuesday of Holy Week, Year C.

Introduction

The events that surround Jesus' approach to Jerusalem, his entry into it, and what happened there are recorded in tumultuous detail by John in his Gospel, as well as by the other three gospel writers. It is clear that Jesus was attracting significant attention, and his presence would likely be giving increasing concern to the Temple authorities. It seems that many people wish to see Jesus.

The Setting

In John's account of Jesus in Jerusalem some familiar threads are reprised. For example, Lazarus' revivification is mentioned (John 12:17), so too is the fact that people who had seen what had happened to Lazarus "continued to testify" and it would seem that others were similarly drawn "to meet him". (12:18) To add to these, the same conclusion as that feared by the Chief Priests and Pharisees (at John 11:48b) is coming to fruition. What is happening is that more "were believing in Jesus" (John 12:11). John's gospel presents us with the picture of a movement gaining in momentum as ". . . the crowd went to meet [Jesus]". In consequence of this the Pharisees, ". . . then said to one another, 'You see, you can do nothing. Look, the world has gone after him!'" (John 12:18-19)

This is where we begin our expository and reflective comment on John 12:20ff. We note that ". . . among those who went up to worship at the festival were some Greeks". Who were they?

Within the spread, the diaspora, were those faithful Jews many of whom spoke Greek. They are referred to here as *Hellenes*, this being the rabbinical, correct, terminology for such a group. Their purpose for being in Jerusalem, we note from the passage, was to worship in the Temple. Like others in Jerusalem at that time they wanted to see Jesus.

From another perspective is the possibility, less plausible in my view, that they actually were Greek Gentiles. Craig Keener, supporting Raymond Brown, argues for this on the basis that Jesus then goes on to exclaim "his hour has come".[2] What is the significance of this, we ask? Well, to explain, Jesus had lived and taught and ministered as a Jew. Now here, so the argument goes, are Gentiles who wish to see him. Citing Josephus, Keener notes that "interested Gentiles would also attend". Whilst this perspective is a thoughtful interpretation of the

---

2 Craig S. Keener, *The Gospel of John; A Commentary*, vol. 2, 871f.

evidence it does not explain why they would also want to take part in worship in a tongue that was not their native one and conceivably in a religion that was also not their own.

Whatever the case, and without detaining ourselves any further on such speculation, everything in John's Gospel has been leading up to the point, the 'hour' as it is called, when all things (Gentile or Jewish) would be fulfilled in Jesus. This is the moment for Jesus to give the teaching that he then gives. When these Greek-speaking worshippers (we need be no more precise than that) ask Philip if they can see (and presumably meet) Jesus we read in the text before us that he then passed the message on to Andrew. The two of them then spoke to Jesus. Whether the worshippers did get to see Jesus is not made clear in the biblical passage. The focus moves on to what Jesus said in the light of their request.

The seed and the fruit

With the arrival of these *Hellenes* Jesus' hour has come. He speaks of his own death using the metaphor of a seed. For it to yield the new growth of a plant, and one that will yield fruit in due time, the seed must cease to be a seed (Jesus speaks of it 'dying' as a seed). It does so because this is what the seed is destined to do. As it ceases to be a seed so a new plant is formed and, when grown, "bears much fruit". (John 12:24) If it doesn't do this it simply remains a seed, unfulfilled, with its reason for existence and its destiny without progression or fulfilment.

We need not apply this metaphor in any literal sense, either to give a more exact botanical correction, nor yet to identify what Jesus meant by 'fruit'. His method of teaching here is in the rabbinical tradition of painting a linguistic picture of a whole scene in order to get his message across about something specific. By doing so he applies the metaphor of the seed to his own forthcoming death. As the seed 'dies' in the ground to yield new life, so he, Jesus, must be lifted up "on the cross" such that in his dying and being laid in the ground a rich harvest for humankind at large may be brought into being. It is his 'glory' that his destiny should be fulfilled by him progressing this way.

This is what is meant by the term, "His hour has come". Jesus' metaphor of the seed dying in the ground to yield fruit from a flourishing tree is his parabolic way of depicting that.

This has wide and significant implications for those who follow Jesus, both then as now.

When I was in seminary extensive teaching was given by our chaplain about losing one's life in order to gain it. Classic spiritual texts such as *Self-Abandonment to Divine Providence*[3] were recommended to resource this theology. The perspective was simple and very attractive to ordination candidates, at least of that era. The basic thesis was that if one cherishes and values who one is now then one loses one's focus on that which ought to be primary, God. As John 12:25 says, "Those who love their life lose it" and by contrast "those who hate their life in this world will keep [in the sense of 'guard' or 'protect'] it for eternal life".

There is much in this teaching that I find appealing, even taking into account some of the regrettable and extreme excesses to which it was given in the mediaeval church, and at other times subsequently, when self-purgation and self-mutilation were the means of its expression. What I am suggesting here is that this teaching, if taken literally, could lead the hapless believer into a life of unhealthy self-mortification in the belief that such behaviour is Christ-like when, in reality, it is not.

Sadly however, it is not difficult to find scriptural passages that do support such extreme readings. Take this for example, "If anyone comes to me [Jesus said] and does not hate his own father and mother and wife and children and brothers and sisters, yes, and even his own life, he cannot be my disciple." (Luke 14:26) Powerful stuff this. And yet it was part of Jesus' method of teaching to exaggerate through hyperbole what he had to say in order, quite deliberately, to get his message across with deliberate force.

The more straightforward application of this teaching is that obedience to God must come before all else in our lives. And when we are confronted by moral dilemmas then it is Christ and obedience to what we perceive his will to be that should guide our action, rather than any personal motivation, preference or bias on our part. By thus following Christ in discipleship, whilst we may well be led into sharing his suffering with him, we are also led into his glory.

What John is offering us in these verses, 12:25-26, is a deliberately focussed choice, securely in the tradition of ancient and classical teaching, between two options. What might this mean? On one side of the issue, we find that sharing in Jesus' suffering will lead one to glory; this we have just recognised. But there is, on the other, a darker side of which we must be careful. Namely

3 Jean Pierre de Caussade, *Self-Abandonment to Divine Providence*, Herder Book Company, St Louis, 1921.

not to inflict suffering on oneself deliberately. This is not what is meant in this scripture. Nor should one look for or expect human praise for being a disciple of Christ; look only to God. The teaching of John 12:25-26 is that in self-denial we will move closer to God in discipleship service. Crucially, self-denial does not, and must never, mean *self-punishment*.

What I am saying here, and the discipline of discipleship that I believe is a necessary part of Christian faith and practice (particularly for Christian leaders) contrasts very markedly with what I hear of clerical formation nowadays. There is an increasing stress on 'my ministry' with correspondingly less emphasis on losing oneself in order to gain new life in God. Equally there is a rising stress on 'me and my rights' as issues of human rights and equality begin to be dominant directives for clergy practice and procedure.

In many ways this modern contextualising of the ordained ministry can be a welcome counter-balance to the heavily ascetic orientation of my seminary days. My comment on this state of affairs is that if the focus in my early days could, and at times did, lead towards unhealthy punishing self-denial, then the current stress on 'me' and 'my' [rights] could become equally damaging unhealthy self-indulgence and self-assertion rather than the ongoing proclamation that "Christ's hour has come". What we must proclaim is *his* hour; not ours.

In short, discipleship ultimately means self-surrender to Christ. This may well mean loss of life and with it all rights and all sense of equality. But the prize is (following John 3:16 and many other passages of scripture) eternal life. Eternal life, in this context, should not be taken to mean something in the future. Living the life of the disciple now means that the life of eternity has already begun for those who do. This theme, both of eternal life, as well as submission to the will of God in discipleship to Jesus, is found in the well-known redemptionist hymn, 'Blessed assurance':

> Blessed assurance, Jesus is mine!
> O what a foretaste of glory divine!
> Heir of salvation, purchase of God;
> born of his Spirit, washed in his blood.
>
> *This is my story, this is my song,*
> *praising my Saviour all the day long,*
> *this is my story, this is my song,*
> *praising my Saviour all the day long.*

31

Perfect submission, perfect delight,
visions of rapture burst on my sight;
angels descending, bring from above
echoes of mercy, whispers of love.

Perfect submission, all is at rest,
I in my Saviour am happy and blest;
watching and waiting, looking above,
filled with his goodness, lost in his love.

Frances van Alstyne [1820-1915] BBC Songs of Praise 288

Jesus in turmoil and Jesus in glory

The verses John 12:27-36, in particular verses 27-28, are John's version of the anguish that Jesus went through, and is reported by the other gospel writers to have taken place, in the Garden of Gethsemane. What John presents us with in his account of those events is a monologue in which Jesus makes three statements:

"Now my soul is troubled"	*he expresses his fear*
"Father, save me from this hour"	*he petitions God for rescue*
"This is why [I] am here now"	*he accepts his lot*

Jesus goes on to ask God to glorify his name and the reply comes that God has already glorified it. There is a fundamental link here between Jesus' suffering and his glory. A detour by means of allegory, probably well known to many, will help us understand what is meant here. The allegory I have in mind is to be found in a remarkable passage mid-way through Jerome K. Jerome's wonderful little book, *Three Men in a Boat.*[4]

By way of background, three pretentious and self-absorbed Englishmen, along with their dog, Montmorency, have been rowing hard upstream on the River Thames towards Runnymede. In one particular sequence they elected to row further than they needed to and so are tired.

A handsomely satisfying meal in the course of that evening comes after a hilariously shambolic effort to erect a cover over their boat. Sleep naturally follows but one of them, awoken by a sharp bit of the boat poking him in the back, goes out for a walk on the river bank. Gazing at the stars his mind enters a reverie.

---

4 Jerome K. Jerome, *Three Men in a Boat* first published 1889, Chapter Ten.

The author of the book, employing rich allegory, narrates this reverie. In it, in what was almost a trance or a mystical experience, he sees horse riders tracing a route along the edge of a forest. One of them wanders into the forest and gets hopelessly lost. His companions press on without him, mourning his loss from their number, but continue nonetheless. They then arrive at their destination, still without their friend, and for several days party and make merry.

In due course their friend does indeed find his way out of the forest and he joins them. He clearly has had a rough time of things for his clothes are ragged and his wounds many. The forest into which he had strayed and through which he had had to find his way had spared him no quarter of respite and offered him no comfort.

He had seen danger, he had seen life's darker side in the forest, and he had expected to die. But, miraculously, he had come through it and as a result was ennobled. The author speaks of the *radiance* on the horse rider's face. This radiance has come to the rider through having had to endure the way of sorrow and grave threat.

This is the point of the story. His companions, satiated to the utmost, are and have been partying their hearts out around a great log fire and are *happy* indeed. Their companion, meanwhile, has come the way of hard travelling by a deeply threatening and soul-injuring route. He, by contrast, is depicted as *radiant.*

Discipleship, with all the likely anguish that comes its way, may not lead to the partying pleasure-ground which the riders enjoyed in full happiness, but it will lead to the radiance displayed by the one who went 'by the way of the dark wood'.

And to develop the allegory, this radiance is the radiance of Christ who came to his glory through this suffering and who offers that same glory, shown in radiance, to all others who go the same way, Christ's way.

Happiness can arise in the here and now, I do not deny that. It can indeed be the outcome of a given life-choice, or maybe be the outcome of a particular political or social objective, but it cannot, I believe, offer the gift of radiance. Radiance, if we interpret it as an allegory of 'glory', as John puts it in his gospel, is a gift from God that comes from enduring with Jesus the way to the cross.

For the disciple of Jesus the radiance that comes with enduring trials, as his disciple, is that one step more towards which each must each aspire. It will not come naturally but is God's gift to those who set their face with him and travel his way of endurance. It involves the discipline of living the holy life of scriptural faithfulness and integrity in prayer.

None of this is ever going to be easy. In the workplace and pleasure-ground there is the ever-ready tendency to follow an easier and more seductively alluring track. But for the one who perforce of circumstances or vocation endures, to continue the allegory, the dangers of the forest and traces the way of discipleship there is reward.

The reward is that of sharing in and reflecting from one's own worn face, nothing other than the radiance of Christ himself. Jesus claimed no glory for himself in this, and neither should we, but said to those around him that what he did was for their sake, not his. (John 12:30)

Judgment and glory

Judgment is a theme not much liked in contemporary western Christian faith. The prevailing preference is that God must be liked and must be likeable. The language one might have been able to use in times past whereby one sees God as a judge is much maligned by many in our day. However, the fact that God does judge is an inescapable fact of faith and we can't, or rather shouldn't, ignore it simply because the term (or what we think the term might mean) does not appeal to modern day predispositions or preferences for comfortable and seemingly unthreatening theology.

Let me summarise to give background context. Jesus is to suffer. He would prefer not to have to. But nonetheless he accepts this will be his fate. And he lets his followers know that if they follow him in discipleship, that what is to happen to him is also likely to happen to them as well. Two key motifs arise for the person of faith: first that suffering may be inevitable and, second, that acceptance of the will of God is necessary.

Paramount, we must stress in all this, was Jesus' concern to do the will of the Father for the sake of the world. It was because of his love for God and out of his love for the world that Jesus condemns (namely, judges) what is wrong in the world and offers the hope of something better than any passing and ephemeral fancy. What is condemned are false seductions that substitute transitory happiness for radiance, misplaced pleasures for the call of discipleship service, and life for the moment rather than life for eternity . . . this list could be developed more or less indefinitely.

Furthermore, the actions and intentions of any one of us who might claim to usurp the authority of God, are set against the standard that Jesus set of selfless self-giving and total abandonment to the will of God. Through his suffering, rejection and death Jesus effected all that God required of his Word in human flesh for the sake of the world. By rising from death, and entering into an eternity of glory with the Father, Jesus demonstrated that even death as the most limiting of human events, in his case as a consequence of the judgment of others, could not restrain him.

By going the way he did Jesus effectively pronounced his judgment, for all time, on those worldly authorities who serve neither God nor his people. The authorities who sought to end Jesus by having him killed, failed. This failure is the indictment and judgment upon them. What is more, Jesus also effectively pronounced his judgment on death's supposed finality by offering life beyond it and, indeed, by opening the way to it for all who go his way. By not holding him in its grasp even death itself is found to have failed. This is the indictment against it.

When Jesus said "while you have the light" he was inviting his followers and all those hearing him to accept his words and to allow their pathway in life to be lit by the light that he was (metaphorically) holding before them so that they too might become sons (and, of course, daughters) of that same light. This was his hope and his calling to them.

Jesus and those listening to him

Meanwhile, those around Jesus had no common mind on what was happening as he stood before them and as God's voice was heard. Some thought it was thunder. Some thought it a voice from an angel. Through it all his hearers still failed to see the significance of what he was saying. I have much sympathy with them for we cannot claim any privileged perception that, had we been in their shoes, we would have done any better. Sadly, the subsequent history of the church demonstrates similar failure of discipleship all too often. The church has failed so many people, so many times. And it has done so even with the advantage of hindsight. The legacy of abuse of vulnerable adults and children by those in breach of ordination vows, monastic vows and of trust is testament to this failure.

Jesus invites his hearers to recognise that the context and place which he and they are in is a place of darkness. He invites them to see that in this darkness he is the light that they will need in order to see meaning and sense in what is happening. Again, this refers to acceptance of unavoidable suffering, should it come about, when brought on by the consequence of living a life of faith. A simple, personal, story will go some way in ordinary human terms towards showing is meant here.

My mother lived a hard life. After successful service in the RAF during the Second World War she married my father. Their life was not an easy one. I have written elsewhere of this and of my father's deeply troubled and troubling manner. As the village post office was at our house there were no secrets about our family's difficulties. Too many people came to our house for the post office, at times when my father was raging, for discretion to prevail.

Knowing of my mother's committed Christian faith, people would ask her how she could believe in God when things were so bad for her. Her unerring reply was that it was only through believing in God that she could cope with her circumstances.

Somehow, just somehow, the acceptance of suffering when it was inevitable, as distinct from being gratuitously self-imposed, led my mother to recognise two things. She spoke not only of what Jesus had done for her in his suffering, but also that he knew what her suffering was like because he too had suffered as a human person. She also knew that, beyond the days of her difficulties, was an eternity in which she would, with her Lord, share in his glory.

It was also the case that she knew even in the most troubled of times that through sharing in the sufferings of Jesus, and of knowing that Jesus shared in hers, she was also sharing in his glory. Of that she had no doubt.

Chapter 4

WEDNESDAY IN HOLY WEEK

Trying to understand Judas Iscariot

A Prayer

O Lord God,
whose blessed Son, our Saviour,
gave his back to the smiters, and did not hide his face from shame:
give us grace to endure the sufferings of this present time,
and confidence in the glory that shall be revealed;
through Jesus Christ our Lord,
who lives and reigns with you,
in the unity of the Holy Spirit,
one God, world without end.
Amen

John 13:21-30
Jesus Foretells His Betrayal

[21]When Jesus had thus spoken, he was troubled in spirit, and testified, "Truly, truly, I say to you, one of you will betray me." [22]The disciples looked at one another, uncertain of whom he spoke. [23]One of his disciples, whom Jesus loved, was lying close to the breast of Jesus; [24]so Simon Peter beckoned to him and said, "Tell us who it is of whom he speaks." [25]So lying thus, close to the breast of Jesus, he said to him, "Lord, who is it?" [26]Jesus answered, "It is he to whom I shall give this morsel when I have dipped it." So, when he had dipped the morsel, he gave it to Judas, the son of Simon Iscariot. [27]Then after the morsel, Satan entered into him. Jesus said to him, "What you are going to do, do quickly." [28]Now no one at the table knew why he said this to him. [29]Some thought that, because Judas had the money box, Jesus was telling him, "Buy what we need for the feast"; or, that he should give something to the poor. [30]So, after receiving the morsel, he immediately went out; and it was night.[1]

---

1 Reading set for Daily Eucharist, Wednesday of Holy Week, Year C (reduced from John 13:21-32).

Introduction

Judas Iscariot has been a vilified and tragic figure from the moment he betrayed Jesus. Without trial and the defence of a fair hearing the church has colluded in a guilty verdict against him. In this chapter I will seek to rehabilitate Judas. The questions will be asked, 'Would we have done anything different had we been him?' and 'Are we so very less guilty than he is?'

The setting

The scene we have before us is of Jesus with his disciples dining. I use the word 'dining' quite deliberately for they would have been together reclining in a large room. Only a large room could accommodate, let us assume, the thirteen of them and also given space for those serving at the meal to move around. By definition almost, a large room is the property of someone able to afford, manage and maintain it.

The setting is, of course, Jerusalem. Those present are together for, quite conceivably, the Passover meal or if not that then a meal of some significance in advance of the Passover. We will hear more about that in the next chapter. And, from verse 23, they are lying down, reclining, for this meal. What might it all have looked like?

We know from elsewhere[2] that those at the meal would have been placed near to others who were their teachers or mentors. Three are known to have been placed on couches at one low table, reclining on the left elbow and eating with the right hand. Others present would have been similarly located at other tables on reclining couches.

Keener notes that in such a setting, "the one to the right of Jesus would need only to lean his head back to find himself near Jesus' chest". Naturally there would have been some sort of precedence in terms of who would have reclined at Jesus' table. The other disciples would have been allotted other places in similar, or closely variant, arrangements. Keener's source material for this is worth citing:

> Romans ate while reclining on couches, usually situated in a U shape (called a *triclinium*) around a low table. The triclinium had places of honor (*sic*) (Luke 14:8-10). Diners supported themselves on their left elbows and ate with their right hands. The ancients did not have forks, only knives

---

2 cf. Keener, *The Gospel of John: A Commentary*, vol. 2, 915.

and spoons. In any event, seated in this position it was more convenient to eat with one's fingers.[3]

Keener also notes the ancient practice of dismissing any other guests as the evening advanced thus allowing the closer group of friends increasing companionship. Such might be particularly the case if a time of significant moment was approaching as was indeed to be the case with Jesus.

Who was with Jesus at his table? From the text we can identify that there were two, this at least bearing out the above arrangement. The one who was "reclining next to him" (13:23) is known only as "the beloved disciple" or as our translation puts it "the one whom Jesus loved". We don't know the identity of this disciple, though forest-loads of paper have been generated by theologians over the centuries on the question. Side-stepping all this history we shall simply let him be known as "the beloved disciple". I will come back to him later. Anyway, Peter motioned over to him, again possibly a suggestion that Peter was at another table, as well as indicating the higher 'status' amongst them of the beloved disciple through whom Peter mediated a question he wished to be put to Jesus.

Peter wanted to know who Jesus was referring to when he said (13:21) that "one of you will betray me". In saying this Jesus was demonstrably troubled, and deeply anxious in his soul. What is more, his words had clearly disturbed all of them. Peter, perhaps as their spokesman, was taking the lead to find out what was meant and used the beloved disciple to ask Jesus who it was that would betray him. The beloved disciple's proximity to Jesus is given by the more literal translation of verse 25, "while leaning on Jesus' chest". The impression is that he leaned back to ask his question.

We are told in the text that the betrayer is indicated in the action of Jesus giving that man the morsel of bread which he had dipped in the dish before him. Did Jesus only give bread to this one disciple? If lying down, as seems certain, in such a position Jesus could almost only have given this piece of bread to one person, namely the one to his left. It was Judas Iscariot. The picture we have therefore is of Jesus at the premier table with, on the one side, the beloved disciple and on the other Judas Iscariot. He is the one whom we know, and who Jesus knows, is to betray him.

---

3 *Ibid.* citing James S. Jeffers *The Greco-Roman World of the New Testament Era: Exploring the Background of Early Christianity*, InterVarsity Press, Downers Grove, Illinois 1999, 39-40.

What is being signified here?

What was the time gap between the beloved disciple posing Peter's question and the giving of the dipped bread? The text of John 13 suggests it was done straightaway. This we can deduce for Jesus says to Judas, "Do quickly what you are going to do". (13:27)

Pausing here for a moment we must note how significant all of this is. The beloved disciple and Judas Iscariot are those who are at, as we would call it, the 'top table' with Jesus. Jesus gave him a piece of bread. Was this, common at the time, a sign of favour? Or might it have been bread dipped in the Haroset (or *charoseth*), the bitter herb sauce of the Passover meal? Either way we cannot tell, but what is clear, and what is often overlooked in readings of this text, is that Judas is almost bidden by Jesus to go and do what he has to do.

The text does not say that Judas sneaked out of the room of his own accord. He was tasked, if that is the right word, to go and do what he had to do, and to get on and do it quickly. John's gospel portrays Judas Iscariot in an unfailingly bad light, and yet, here at the moment of leaving the group of disciples in the intimacy of friends dining together, he only goes when Jesus bids him leave to do so.

In this action, it is almost as if Jesus gives him permission to go to his task. From John 10:17ff. Jesus speaks of his life that "no one takes it from him; he lays it down freely".

To enable Judas Iscariot to carry out his intention to betray Jesus the text tells us that Satan entered into him. This is an interesting image. It contrasts markedly with that of the Holy Spirit of God entering into Jesus at his baptism in Mark's gospel and of the Holy Spirit similarly lighting upon the disciples at the first Pentecost. Whilst such imagery may seem uncommon in our secularising times, picturing divine, and other 'spiritual' interventions, was familiar in the Mediterranean world of Jesus' time.

I read a recent book review in a theological journal when the reviewer said of the particular book under her examination that if we were uneasy in this modern age of speaking about Satan (or the Devil, however denoted) that we could simply substitute 'evil'. In one sense this is correct for 'evil' is indeed a close companion in kind to Satanic or Demonic evil. For myself, and I believe being true to the biblical text, I do not accept that we should so easily remove the reality of Satan. I have now been ordained thirty-nine years and at several times in the ministry that has come to me I have encountered and resisted real Satanic, Demonic, forces. I share the view of others who have experience in what is called deliverance ministry that such powers of darkness should neither be minimised nor yet given an exaggerated status they do not deserve.

Let me share one example to illustrate this.

At a church with which I was once involved two members of the congregation were observed and heard chanting demonic incantations during a Christmas Day morning communion. One of them was joined by another for the same sort of activity on Easter Day. The priest of that church with others in the congregation undertook, in consultation with me, what amounted to a simple exorcism of the building. The people who had done those incantations left the congregation. Initially the congregation numbers dipped, but as I write this, numbers are rising, the church has been cleansed and is now bright, light and busy. Where once that church was dark and decaying (flowers were rarely refreshed, clutter was being allowed to accumulate in quantities, filth was on the increase) in so many ways the fresh air of the Holy Spirit now moves freely through it. The simple exorcism was followed by a full renovation of the inside of the church. All now is new and fresh. Both the place and the people.

The bible does not shy away from speaking of the destructive power of Satan. Nor does it shy away from affirming the power and light of Christ to counter, decisively, any power of darkness there might be. This imagery can be developed a little further with other biblical reference and applications.

We recognise, for example, that the Gospel of John contrasts light and dark at a number of places in its narrative. In the Prologue of the Gospel in Chapter One it reads, ". . . in him was light, and the light was the light of the world . . ." In betrayal, Judas Iscariot left during the darkness of night. The symbolism is deeply poignant. John's terse wording of this (13:30) highlights the drama, "And it was night."

A further contrast can be drawn between this drama and the Passover meal as recorded in the other three gospels and Paul's First Letter to the Corinthians. In each Jesus was at the Passover meal with his disciples. In each he shared bread with them (and wine) to signify that through their continuation of this meal they were to remember who Jesus was. In the tradition that John records for us in his account of what, admittedly, I am taking to be the Passover meal, it is Judas who is remembered. This is so because of his betrayal. For the earliest church the significance of this would be poignant. Equally so for us.

And still the disciples misunderstood

While all this drama was unfolding the disciples still failed to see the significance of what Jesus said, and of his action in giving Judas Iscariot the piece of bread. What did they say amongst themselves? Opinion in their group was divided between the thought that Judas was going to buy provisions for the forthcoming Passover or, conversely, was on his way to give alms to the poor. For either of these Judas, as the purse-bearer, would have been the appropriate person to send. As it was his intention was neither honourable nor charitable.

Judas Iscariot was vilified by the Gospel writers, who as their texts were prepared, knew the outcome. They record that Jesus had stern words to say of him. Going down through the centuries we find that Dante committed Judas to the innermost and final circle of hell for his betrayal of Jesus. Not for Judas the torment of the more lenient sulphurous flames, the punishment set for misplaced lust and passion; for Judas it was to be the coldest ice of frozen rigidity, at the complete mercy of Lucifer's eternal torture.[4] The greatest punishments in hell, as envisaged in Dante's schema, were reserved for "sins of deceit against those we have cause to trust".

Throughout history Judas has been, and in many ways remains, a vilified figure. In the rock musical of the 1960s and 1970s *Jesus Christ Superstar* Judas Iscariot was played by a black actor, deliberately contrasting with the otherwise all white cast. And at the end of the film version of the musical he is seen running alone into oblivion being chased by a horizon of armoured tanks. Judas the betrayer is the black outsider and is portrayed as the guilt-loaded scapegoat pursued over the centuries by overwhelming odds with little or no defence at his disposal.

Surely this cannot be right. Though betrayal by a friend is most heinously awful perhaps we too, like those disciples in conversation over their communal meal, have misunderstood Judas Iscariot. Judas is, I suggest, only a hairs-breadth different from Peter. Remember it was to be Peter who, three times, would deny Jesus. He lived onwards after his denials to be able to affirm Jesus as Lord. To match his threefold denial his subsequent affirmation was similarly thrice.

And don't forget the other disciples in the Garden of Gethsemane as those tasked to arrest Jesus got ready to go there and take him. Three of

4 Dante *The Inferno*, cf particularly Canto 34:10-12 and 52-63, with 'That one up there, condemned to greater pain, is Judas Iscariot,' my teacher said . . . (61-62).

these disciples, at least, were asked by Jesus to stay awake with him one hour. What happened? They went to sleep. Just at the moment when most they were needed by the anguished Jesus they dozed. They, with Peter, went on to live another day. Judas did not. He could not live with his failure, whereas it would seem the others could.

Judas, having betrayed his friend, then killed himself. Was his action remorse, guilt, appalling realisation of fault? Yes, any of these and more. On this basis, it takes but a little step in thinking that his suicide was an honourable, even if tragic, exit for a saddened and crestfallen man.

Here's why. Adam, as in Adam and Eve from the Old Testament Book of Genesis, is the classic person who gets things wrong. Adam isn't so much a person who lived once in history. Rather he is you and me, who live in history now. We get it wrong. We mess up. We are deceived by others like us. And we allow ourselves to be deceivers as well. We fail to tell the truth. We fail to do what is right; even when we intend otherwise. And, given all this, given all the things that we might do which are right, any one of us could have been, might even now be, the person who betrayed, and continues to betray, Jesus. Not to put too fine a point on it, someone had to betray Jesus and to engineer the means by which he could be handed over to those who sought his end. This necessary action had to have someone to perform it. A flawed and fallible human being, like you and me, was needed to do the deed that had to be done.

Adam is any one of us and is all of us. Likewise, so is Judas. For this reason, there is enigma in the figure of Judas. If through the centuries the church has wrongfully, in my view, pilloried this hapless figure so now, at the furthest extreme of Judas' rehabilitation, is his arrival as a fateful attraction. Here is what I mean by this.

Lady Gaga, in her album track 'Judas', sings of him as her lover. As she does so she sees herself as a Mary Magdalene figure washing Judas' feet with her hair as though he were Jesus. She says she will remain his lover even after his betrayal of her three times over. This motif echoes Jesus' attitude to Peter after his threefold denial. Lady Gaga sees Judas as a king with no crown.

Lady Gaga, in 'Judas' develops the ambiguity of love for such a man as Judas. Love, she has learned is like a brick, it can help build a house, or it can add weight to someone drowning. In her own sinfulness she admits, and whilst almost delighting in it, there is the sign of a lament; "Jesus is her virtue; Judas is her vice". She lusts for him and for vice. Would that it were, let me add personally and from my own perspective, that her desire had been for virtue as given in Jesus.

Now, I must say, without equivocation, that I find many of Lady Gaga's lyrics in most of her songs, utterly abhorrent. My reason for reflecting on her words about Judas is simply to highlight her extreme and magnetic fascination with a man that the church has vilified for multiples of centuries and who is, as you are perhaps guessing from the way I am writing, now being recovered as someone not very different from you or me. Someone who has been perpetually misunderstood, just as Judas was by the disciples of old.

In the end we have no real alternative, I believe, but to view Judas Iscariot as the person any of us could have been. He made one mistake and because he could not live with it, in death that mistake has been held against him ever since. Over almost two thousand years he has been condemned without either fair trial or fair hearing.

Beyond his sketchy appearances in the gospels, and in this one action of betrayal and his subsequent death, we know little else about him. Nothing about his childhood, his family relationships, any illness or tormented personality he might have had and so on. In saying this, however, we must be on guard not to let Judas off the hook too easily, for what he did was wrong. But by admitting he had done wrong, even if took him to his suicide he too, like you and me, deserves the option, nay, the benefit of God's forgiveness and our latter-day compassionate understanding.

Richard Bauckham and Trevor Hart see Judas Iscariot's action this way:

> Viewed from a human angle Judas's action is a crass betrayal of one who loved him. Viewed in the wider theological context, his action is not excused of its moral orientation but is subsumed under that which had to take place, and that which God intended *should* take place, in order that the sins of his people might be forgiven".[5]

In the action of Judas through the wrongdoing of betrayal the purpose of Jesus could be fulfilled. Jesus needed 'a Judas' and, it seems, this particular Judas did not let him down.

Judas died. He killed himself. His death prevented him from seeing the resurrection. It prevented him from being on the beach with the others for

---

5 Richard Bauckham and Trevor Hart, *At the Cross*, Darton, Longman and Todd, London 1999, 18.

the fish breakfast that the risen Jesus later on cooked for his friends and when he assured Peter of the new-found forgiven trajectory which henceforth would be his. His death prevented the possibility of that open repentance of sin that might surely have come to him.

In conclusion

I have referred to the Lady Gaga song, 'Judas', above. More poignantly and more agreeably (to my sensibility at least) is another song, Ruth Etchells' *Ballad of the Judas Tree*. In its universalist theme she muses imaginatively upon the relationship between Jesus and the forgiven Judas in heaven. Powerful are its words as Jesus is portrayed going into Hell to rescue Judas. Perhaps it is with this vision that I prefer to see Judas in eternity. Not in the iced condemnation assigned him by Dante but rather that he is rescued in the arms of a forgiving and loving Jesus who went into Hell to redeem even the one who betrayed him; the one who had not been able to live with the consequences of what he had done.

THE JUDAS TREE[6]

In Hell there grew a Judas Tree
Where Judas hanged and died
Because he could not bear to see
His master crucified

Our Lord descended into Hell
And found his Judas there
For ever hanging on the tree
Grown from his own despair

So Jesus cut his Judas down
And took him in his arms
"It was for this I came" he said
"And not to do you harm

My Father gave me twelve good men
And all of them I kept
Though one betrayed and one denied
Some fled and others slept

In three days' time I must return
To make the others glad
But first I had to come to Hell
And share the death you had

My tree will grow in place of yours
Its roots lie here as well
There is no final victory
Without this soul from Hell"

So when we all condemned him
As of every traitor worst
Remember that of all his men
Our Lord forgave him first

D. Ruth Etchells

---

6 Cited from Bauckham and Hart, *op. cit.*, 20-21.

Chapter 5
MAUNDY THURSDAY
Jesus' final meal with his followers

A Prayer

O God our Father,
as you invite us to share in the supper that your Son
gave to his Church to proclaim his death until he comes:
inspire us by his service,
and unite us in his love;
who lives and reigns with you,
in the unity of the Holy Spirit,
one God, world without end.
Amen

John 13:1-7, 31-35
Jesus Washes the Disciples' Feet

[1]Now before the feast of the Passover, when Jesus knew that his hour had come to depart out of this world to the Father, having loved his own who were in the world, he loved them to the end. [2]And during supper, when the devil had already put it into the heart of Judas Iscariot, Simon's son, to betray him, [3]Jesus, knowing that the Father had given all things into his hands, and that he had come from God and was going to God, [4]rose from supper, laid aside his garments, and girded himself with a towel. [5]Then he poured water into a basin, and began to wash the disciples' feet, and to wipe them with the towel with which he was girded. [6]He came to Simon Peter; and Peter said to him, "Lord, do you wash my feet?" [7]Jesus answered him, "What I am doing you do not know now, but afterward you will understand."

The New Commandment

[31]When [Judas] had gone out, Jesus said, "Now is the Son of man glorified, and in him God is glorified; [32]if God is glorified in him, God will also glorify him in himself, and glorify him at once. [33]Little children, yet a little while I am with you. You will seek me; and as I

said to the Jews so now I say to you, 'Where I am going you cannot come.' [34]A new commandment I give to you, that you love one another; even as I have loved you, that you also love one another. [35]By this all men will know that you are my disciples, if you have love for one another."[1]

---

1 Reading set for Daily Eucharist, Maundy Thursday, Years A,B and C (reduced and adapted from John 13:1-17, 31b-35).

Introduction

The picture of Jesus with his disciples at the last supper is very much coloured by traditional artistic representations; not least Michaelangelo's in a the refectory of a former convent adjoining the Basilica di Santa Maria delle Grazie in Milan. The setting may well, and as I will argue below, not have looked like that at all. In this chapter we enter the world of hospitality traditions and customs normal in Jesus' day. We also encounter the extravagance of Jesus washing the disciples' feet as an act of utterly unexpected servility. By so abasing himself he elevated the duty of service to others as a means of giving glory to God.

The Setting

This passage of scripture is the reading from the gospel for the service in churches on Maundy Thursday. At the heart of this gospel passage is Jesus washing the feet of his disciples. This is a wonderfully familiar reading and it deserves our serious attention. Let me therefore begin with an obvious question: 'why was foot washing practised?'[2] Some background material will help us understand what happened that evening in Jerusalem.

Many streets at that time would have been poorly constructed, narrow probably, crowded with people and dirty with dog mess and human waste material. Even if Jesus was dining with his disciples in a wealthier part of town, he and the others would have had to have walked there through other streets. There would be dust, filth of all sorts and everything that might be unpleasant on their feet even if they'd been wearing sandals.

There are multiple examples from ancient Judaic practice of water being brought to enable foot-washing. Here are a few, "Let a little water be brought, and wash your feet, and rest yourselves . . ." The same occurs when Lot welcomes the 'angelic' visitors in Genesis 19:2 and in the hospitable welcome of Laban to Abraham's servant (Genesis 24:32). The task of washing another's feet would fall to the servant, or a child, or, as in the case of Abigail, a wife who assumes in her duty as a wife the servant and slave roles in one move, "[Abigail] rose and bowed down, with her face to the ground, and said, 'Your

2 This chapter is substantially the same, though with some adaptations and some additions, as one in my *Three Days in Holy Week*, Handsel Press, Edinburgh 2014, 6-13. That chapter, in turn, was based on a sermon I gave in St Thomas' Episcopal Church, Fifth Avenue, New York City, on Maundy Thursday 2012.

servant is a slave to wash the feet of the servants of my lord.'"[3] The home owner, or host, would not however have been the one to do the washing. The situation of Abigail is mirrored in 1 Timothy 5:10 in respect of the 'widow', ". . . she must be well attested for her good works, as one who has brought up children, shown hospitality, washed the saints' feet, helped the afflicted, and devoted herself to doing good in every way."

So then, and following Craig Keener, we accept the custom of washing the feet of guests on arrival at someone's home as normal. We also accept that at the time it was also the 'done thing' when one returns home. Additionally it was a conventional social custom both to welcome someone and to help them feel at home when they appeared at one's door. Offering water for foot washing was therefore accepted hospitality.

Keener quotes his own principal source regarding foot washing, John C. Thomas, who says that Jesus' act of foot washing represents "the most menial task", being "unrivalled in antiquity."[4] He also cites foot washing as practised both in Greek and Roman custom as well as "in cultic settings in early Jewish sources".[5]

Quite apart from anything else, foot washing would have been a common-sense thing to do. Quite clearly it was important to make sure that what is stuck to you from the street doesn't get spread around the house. Water was normally plentiful in Jerusalem. The task therefore was easily straightforward given where Jesus and the disciples were.

The meal in Jerusalem

John 13 sees Jesus and his disciples meeting in Jerusalem for a meal. Interestingly Jesus isn't the owner of the room where he and the disciples are meeting for this meal. We do not know who was. Washing upon arrival would have been ensured by the person whose home it was. The potential for offence would have been real if there hadn't been a foot-washing on arrival. From elsewhere in the gospels, ". . . I [Jesus] entered your house; you gave me no water for my feet, but she has bathed my feet with her tears and dried them with her hair."[6]

---

3 1 Samuel 25:41.

4 Craig Keener, *The Gospel of John: A Commentary,* vol. 2, 904 citing *Foot washing in John 13 and the Johannine Community,* JSNT Supplement 61, Sheffield Academic Press, Sheffield 1991.

5 Craig Keener, *The Gospel of John: A Commentary,* vol. 2, 902-3.

6 Luke 7:44.

Jesus is in Jerusalem for this meal. He has his disciples around him. He was what we would call the head of the table at that meal even though not the owner of the house where it was taking place. What might this gathering have looked like?

As we noted in the previous chapter, those at the meal would be lying down. Their position would have been reclining on one elbow, probably eating their food with their right hand fingers with a low table before them and their feet outwards away from the table. Those serving them would be standing and walking about. In all conceivability Jesus and the disciples might well have been grouped at separate low tables.

The foot-washing

The scriptures record that "Jesus rose", that is to say he stood up, left the centre of the meal, went to its outer edge where everyone's feet were and with the towel around his waist would have used a bowl and washed their feet with both hands available.

In this setting Jesus, despite Peter's protest at the time, bathed the disciples' feet as they reclined at table and whilst the meal was taking its course and was, it would seem, well on the way towards completion. Peter's objection to what Jesus was doing was based on the norm that Jesus should not be doing this most menial of actions. Rather, Peter says, it would be better for him to be doing it. Peter was probably employing hyperbole here, for at the same time as protesting that he should be the one doing the foot washing, he would be thinking it was too demeaning for anyone other than the lowest servant or slave to have to do.

The point of Jesus' reply, including the words at v. 14 ". . . you also ought to wash one another's feet" was that if Peter was not prepared to wash the feet of others (that is, to become the servant of all) then neither should he expect to be able to sit at the table of Jesus. Peter, again no doubt employing hyperbole with a possible hint at ridicule of Jesus for what he was doing, asked for a full body wash, ". . . not my feet only but also my hands and my head".

In terms of social custom there was no need for this. Peter knew it. So too did Jesus. Peter had been washed on arrival at the house. That would have been done and repetition was unnecessary. What Jesus was now doing in the foot washing, during the meal, was something more. It was, and remains, the 'extra mile' of discipleship.

This can also be read in a further and complementary way.

The 'word' of Jesus, spoken to the disciples (see 15:3, "You have already been cleansed by the word that I have spoken to you"), has already cleansed them thoroughly and completely. This is metaphorical language, but its meaning is clear. Right now and before them, as this meal is coming towards its close, they are being "offered something over and beyond that benefit".[7]

What Jesus was doing in the foot washing was quite deliberately to turn the social customs of the day upside down. Yes he was the greatest. So therefore he made himself the least by doing what he did, when he did it, and by the way he did it. Peter's language of protest whilst this was happening is linguistically emphatic. His words begin with 'Lord' and end with 'feet', from the highest to the lowest quite literally, anatomically, from top to toe.

So by washing their feet Jesus was doing more than what was expected. Those there had already been welcomed. Food had already been prepared and presented. Now Jesus was doing something more. He was trying to teach the disciples something extra.

Jesus' action was deliberately one which emphasised the virtue of humility. Jesus was leading by example. Such would normally have been respected by those around in the right context and when performed by those instructed to carry it out. On this occasion Peter did not comprehend what was happening. That said, his loyalty to Jesus cannot be denied and nor can his desire to protect the position of Jesus as their teacher and leader.

Examples of someone showing humility towards others would have been familiar enough to everyone at the time. But what Jesus did on this occasion is to take the position of a slave, the lowest person, when he did the washing. Even those who would have been prepared to adopt a position of humility would never have bent so low as to do what Jesus did in this context, especially after the meal when such an act would not have been expected or required. What Jesus did was not only unexpected it was, in fact, unthinkable!

Peter's lack of understanding at Jesus' actions came about because what Jesus did went beyond even the conventions of humility. Craig Keener notes that "adopting postures of slavery must have been rare".[8]

Next, what Jesus did in the foot washing could be interpreted as a cleansing of sin and a motif for faith, being 'washed by Jesus'. Verse 10

---

7 Charles H. Talbert *Reading John*, SPCK, London 1992, 192.
8 Keener, 907.

suggests that Jesus recognises this in those around him, "One who has bathed does not need to wash, except for the feet, but is entirely clean."[9]

We have already noted the cleansing power of the 'word' of Jesus. In addition to that there could be an allusion here to the disciples' ritual purification before a Passover meal, alongside the need for a further washing, such as is being given here, to prepare them for discipleship service. I will return to this theme very shortly.

An example to follow

What Jesus has done for his followers they should similarly imitate and do for others. As they do this so they will be aligning themselves with his proclamation of, and living out, the kingdom of God. Interweaving the motif of loving service with suggestions of the betrayal links this action of Jesus with his coming conviction and sentencing to death. In what Jesus did he was prefiguring the humiliation he will shortly have to face in his dying. By indicating that the disciples should wash one another's feet Jesus was laying out before them the cost of discipleship. Craig Keener again notes, ". . . it seems clear that John invites us to read the foot washing in view of the cross."[10] For the followers of Jesus discipleship must always involve sacrifice and service.

By offering the teaching that he gave from v. 12 onwards ("After he had washed their feet, had put on his robe, and had returned to the table . . .") Jesus was asserting his authority as a teacher amongst them. In who he was Jesus was giving instruction, and displaying by example, a level of discipleship which they could not have anticipated, nor would they have been looking for it. By following Jesus' teaching and by following his example they would be "blessed" (v. 17).

As we look at other ancient sources there is material where the term 'having unwashed feet' also means 'not being prepared'. This leads us to ask another question. Did this mean that in the action of Jesus washing his disciples' feet mean he was preparing them for something else . . . for a more significant form of discipleship beyond that which they had already experienced? Preparing them for trials ahead? Preparing them for the day when they would enter their Father's home? Preparing them for discipleship when they too would have to overturn norms of accepted practice and

---

9 Some ancient texts omit "except for the feet".
10 Keener, 907.

conventions of seniority and privilege in their loving discipleship service of others? It is very possible.

From a different perspective, and because of his union with the Father, Jesus was also their host at this meal in a different sense and, in himself, was their gateway to all that was to follow, heaven included. In readiness for their entry to it he, as their heavenly host, welcomed them by offering the customary earthly ritual of foot washing. This is a simple preparation for all that is to come the way of the disciples. It is also a foretaste of the heavenly banquet that is prepared for those who follow his way; both the disciples then and us now.

How much of this the disciples realised at the time we can never know. I suspect it was not very much. The meaning and significance of Jesus' actions, as well as of his teaching, would not have been clear to them in that hour. Only later would the penny drop.

In going away

Verses 31-35 of John 13 should strictly follow the section where Jesus has instructed Judas Iscariot to go and do what he has to do. For our purposes here they are inserted after Jesus' exchanges with Peter. Either way there is no violence to the text by this 'cut and paste' for Jesus has to prepare his disciples for what has to come next both for them and for him. He does this within a long discourse and reflective meditation on what is to happen to him as well as an exhortation to them about their life as disciples and what this means. What he says begins at 13:31 and continues all the way through to 17:26.

There is no overall clear structure to this long section. Themes appear, are overtaken by others, and then reappear later. A parallel can be drawn with the structure of a musical score where the composer introduces a particular motif, allows it to develop, and then returns to its origin, it later having weaved in other themes and textures along the way. My one-time Professor of New Testament at the University of Edinburgh said to us undergraduates that this passage should be 'sung rather than analysed'. For someone as un-musical as I am it is always helpful to have a piece of literature such as John's Gospel likened to a totally different genre in order for its meaning and richness to be helpfully brought forward.

In this short section, taken from Jesus' long passage of teaching, we have him seeking to give comfort to his disciples that though he is going away, and to his death, all of it is within God's plan for him and for the universe. Even though Judas Iscariot has gone out into the night to betray Jesus, and even though Jesus has self-abased himself in the action of foot-washing nonetheless he is now glorified. No action however unworthy, or however servile, can detract from this. Even though the disciples could not understand this at the time when they heard it (and the theme of 'glory' in John's gospel is a repeating one) nonetheless the day would come when the meaning of all that they had heard from Jesus would come clear, in particular the various emphases he chose to repeat time and again. It was therefore not a failure that they were unable to understand him. Sometimes good teaching is given at a particular point deliberately with its relevance and meaning only to emerge later.

What Jesus said to his followers was given in private conversation and for all that we know it continued around the table or tables where they were assembled for the meal in Jerusalem. 'Farewell speeches' like this were familiar in the Judaism of Jesus' day.[11] Talbert places such speeches in four categories:

(1) A noteworthy figure knows he is about to die, gathers his primary community about him and tells them . . .

(2) The hero gives a farewell speech to his primary community that includes a prediction of the future . . .

(3) The farewell speech also contains an exhortation about how to behave after the hero has departed . . .

(4) The farewell speech with its predictions and exhortations sometimes closes with a prayer for those the hero is leaving behind . . .[12]

All these features characterise John 13:31 – 17:26.

In the little section of five verses we are looking at here Jesus contrasts the glory that is his, with the humiliation of his forthcoming arrest and trial as well as with the servility he has shown in the washing of his disciples' feet. To this we can add also the ultimate degrading experience that was crucifixion. Despite each intimation to the contrary Jesus is being glorified. In his defeat there is victory. In his weakness there is strength. And so on.

As, paradoxically, Jesus is glorified in all this so the glory is also that of God the Father. And Jesus would have no glory at all (unless he were to claim a flawed human-based glory) were it not that the Father was placing his glory upon him.

---

11   Cf. Charles H. Talbert, *Reading John*, SPCK, London 1992, 200f. for a comprehensive summary of this.
12 Talbert, 200-201.

In familiar terms Jesus addresses his followers as 'children' (13:33) a common descriptor based on active friendship roles as well as to teacher–disciple relationships. In this particular discourse Jesus is preparing them for his death, something that would not be long in the coming. Any similar fate for them would arise, if it were to do so, later. As things were when he said this, he would be with them in person for, "just a little while" longer. (13:33)

A new commandment

This is given to the disciples by Jesus. They are to, "love one another, just as [he] has loved [them] . . ."(13:34) With the example of him having washed their feet so fresh in their experience the meaning of this could barely have been more self-evident. It was by following his example, shared with them, that they would continue the most foundational aspect of his self-giving life once Jesus had gone. By so doing they would, as Craig Keener puts it, ". . . continue to experience his love".[13] For those who are familiar with the Holy Communion service in today's church the words "Do this in remembrance of me" will resonate loudly. Although in the Communion service these words refer most specifically to sharing in the bread and the wine, their extension to self-giving service for others cannot be either denied or ignored in the duty of the practising Christian.

It must be noted that loving one another does not imply, or rather should never be taken to imply, hostility towards others. Love within the Christian community is that example, and the principal means, by which those outside Christian faith and practice see what being a disciple of Christ means. Where those who profess to be Christians fail to show love to another person, whoever that person might be, and for whatever serious or avoidably minor action they might take (such as not giving up a cherished seat in church) then the witness of Christian faith is denied and, ultimately, Christ himself is once more betrayed.

This may seem a hard teaching. But in the end I see no alternative. When Christians bicker and bluster with one another (most often over utter trivialities) then nothing less than the word of God is being denied and so too is the missional evangelism that God demands of us.

Let me offer, as this chapter closes and as I have done in each of the chapters of this book, something from the world of music and invite your contemplative focus on the emphasised words that follow. This motet by S.S.

---

13 Keener, 923.

Wesley[14] is a deeply moving and highly evocative composition. Its beauty in its words is matched to the full in the sympathetic beauty of the music that accompanies it.

Blessed be the God and Father of our Lord Jesus Christ,
which according to his abundant mercy
hath begotten us again unto a lively hope
by the resurrection of Jesus Christ from the dead,
To an inheritance incorruptible, and undefiled,
that fadeth not away,
reserved in heaven for you,
Who are kept by the power of God
through faith unto salvation
ready to be revealed at the last time.

But as he which hath called you is holy,
so be ye holy in all manner of conversation.
Pass the time of your sojourning here in fear.

Love one another with a pure heart fervently.
See that ye love one another.
Love one another with a pure heart fervently:

Being born again,
not of corruptible seed,
but of incorruptible,
by the word of God.

For all flesh is as grass,
and all the glory of man
as the flower of grass.
The grass withereth,
and the flower thereof falleth away.

But the word of the Lord endureth for ever.
Amen.   [1 Peter 1:3-5, 15, 22-25]

---

14 The internet offers easy facility to listen to this and other music that I have cited. The emphasised words echo the theme of this chapter.

Chapter Six
GOOD FRIDAY
The approach to the cross

A Prayer
Almighty Father,
look with mercy on this your family:
for which our Lord Jesus Christ was willing to be betrayed,
given up into the hands of sinners, and to suffer death upon the cross;
who lives and reigns with you, in the unity of the Holy Spirit,
one God, world without end.
Amen

John 18: 1-11
The Betrayal and Arrest of Jesus

[1]When Jesus had spoken these words, he went forth with his disciples across the Kidron valley, where there was a garden, which he and his disciples entered. [2]Now Judas, who betrayed him, also knew the place; for Jesus often met there with his disciples. [3]So Judas, procuring a band of soldiers and some officers from the chief priests and the Pharisees, went there with lanterns and torches and weapons. [4]Then Jesus, knowing all that was to befall him, came forward and said to them, "Whom do you seek?" [5]They answered him, "Jesus of Nazareth." Jesus said to them, "I am he." Judas, who betrayed him, was standing with them. [6]When he said to them, "I am he," they drew back and fell to the ground. [7]Again he asked them, "Whom do you seek?" And they said, "Jesus of Nazareth." [8]Jesus answered, "I told you that I am he; so, if you seek me, let these men go." [9]This was to fulfil the word which he had spoken, "Of those whom thou gavest me I lost not one." [10]Then Simon Peter, having a sword, drew it and struck the high priest's slave and cut off his right ear. The slave's name was Malchus. [11]Jesus said to Peter, "Put your sword into its sheath; shall I not drink the cup which the Father has given me?"[1]

---

1 Reading set for Daily Eucharist, Good Friday, Years A,B and C (shortened from John 18: 1 – 19: 42).

Introduction

Good Friday is the day when, for obvious reasons, the Christian Church remembers the death of Jesus by crucifixion. Worship in churches around the world revolves around the remembering and observance of that event. However, in what follows I am choosing to consider the events that John records as having taken place at the arrest of Jesus. My reason for doing so takes into account the simple fact that in two other devotional books, similar to this one in style that I have written for Holy Week and Good Friday, I placed considerable focus on the crucifixion[2]. What you will find below is material that is new to me and, insofar as the arrest of Jesus led to his crucifixion a few hours later, its inclusion is appropriate for a book with the title that you now have in your hands.

The setting

Towards the end of the last chapter I introduced the long section of teaching that Jesus shared with his disciples and which fills the whole of John's Gospel from Chapter 13, verse 31 to Chapter 17, verse 26. My starting point for what now follows begins at the end of that long teaching section where the writer of John's Gospel records, "After Jesus had spoken these words..." (18:1a) The narrative then picks up where Jesus and his disciples leave the Temple Mount in Jerusalem, descend the Kidron valley, cross the stream, and enter a garden, an olive grove, on the other side of it. It is here that Jesus is to be arrested and it is to this that our attention is now drawn.

In many respects, John's account of the arrest of Jesus, and of the events preceding it, is at one and the same time both somewhat different from and yet is strikingly similar to the other three gospels. It is quite conceivable that John had heard how the arrest of Jesus had taken place because several there would each have their own account of the events to share. These accounts would have been circulating amongst Jesus' followers, not least because in each gospel various of them are given as having been there. In all likelihood, John had his own sources upon which to base what he wrote down and may, in addition, also have had his own eyewitness testimony to draw upon.

---

2 Robert A. Gillies, with Helen Firth and Richard Scotcher, *Sounds before the Cross*, Handsel Press, Edinburgh 2007 and *Three Days in Holy Week*, Handsel Press, Edinburgh 2014.

Likewise, John, we can see from the text, had particular emphases which he wished to highlight and to which the events of Jesus' death particularly spoke. Accordingly, and on these bases, he painted in words the narrative of Jesus' death that has subsequently been offered to posterity as the Gospel that bears his name. In doing so he had available to him both that which he had heard from others as well as his own likely first-hand experience.[3]

Amongst these emphases are Jesus' words to the soldiers who came for him, "I am he" (18:5), as well as the overall picture of Jesus that is portrayed in this section where he is presented as being in full control of the unfolding drama. John's Jesus is not the anxiety-ridden Jesus in Gethsemane of Matthew, Mark or Luke who with tears pleads that "this cup be taken from him". No; John presents Jesus, fully consistent with the remainder of his Gospel, as one who freely took hold of life and as one who freely lays it down. I shall return to this shortly.

For the moment, however, it is important to say a little about how different texts, such as the gospels, can say the same things about the same events but in different ways. A recent example from my own experience will, I trust, help to illustrate the point. My subheading for the next section points to what I mean.

Four gospels; one message

Early in January 2016 very severe rain caused extensive flooding in the small town of Ballater in the upper Deeside area of Aberdeenshire. It was not the only place affected by flooding. Aboyne further downstream on the Dee was also badly affected as were a number of villages on the Dee's tributaries. Likewise, Port Elphinstone and parts of Inverurie on the River Don were similarly under water. The damage both to businesses and to homes was extensive with recovery forecast to last into multiples of months. As, indeed, it did.

I visited Ballater over a two-day period in the week following the flood. I spoke to people clearing up amidst the damage to their saturated homes and helped carry possessions into the street for collection and summary disposal. I visited businesses. And I visited the homes of people who had had no damage and who wondered how or why they had been spared. Gardens were wrecked, cars destroyed and 'sink holes', as they are called, pot-marked the roads. In every situation everyone had their story to tell of what had

---

3 In making the assertion that John was a first-hand witness of the events I am referring to I am very much indebted to the insights of my friend, and former member of my previous congregation, Richard Bauckham.

happened. Everyone's story was unique. Each was different. And yet each was true for each one of them truly described a particular aspect of what had happened as well as pointing to the reality of the whole event.

I was back in Ballater two months later, and in Aboyne also. In a small gathering of people from the two communities still the stories of that horrendous flood were being told. They needed to be told. For when people experience a great tragedy the need to recount what happened is essential. It is part of the process of eventual healing. Once more I heard stories, again each was individually true, but every one of which was different from all the others I had heard previously. But yet they all recounted and referred to the same totally recognisable and identifiable situation. In this case it was a flood. But, in the Jerusalem of some two thousand years ago, it could have so easily been the betrayal, arrest, trial, torture and death of a beloved friend.

Each person involved would tell their own story of what happened. Each person's story would have differences from the others and yet the similarities between each of them would point to and be part of the reality towards which the truth of their story pointed.

As regards Jesus, the question could be asked if his followers had invented the story. If they had done so they would with all certainty have made sure all the discrepancies were ironed out if they had wanted, artificially, to make the story stick.

What is more, why would they even have wanted to invent such a story or to keep on recounting the events of the arrest and death of Jesus? There was already enough 'Jesus trouble' around for them to seek to create more bother when, if it had all been a fabrication, there would have been no need to add to it. In summary, there was no need for the early Christians to fabricate a story, or to keep repeating a narrative, that would likely bring them yet further trouble from the Roman occupying force, and from the Temple authorities.

They didn't have to invent a falsehood to bring them yet more bother. They could have kept their heads down and kept quiet. But they couldn't and they didn't. Each of them had to tell the story of their friend as they had experienced it; of how Jesus died and, *crucially,* of him rising. It was his rising that gave meaning to the events of the crucifixion and to all that had preceded it. And tell it they did. It is human nature to do so. And given their later experience of Jesus' resurrection they needed to do so in order to speak of the victory that God won through Jesus' arrest, torture, dying and death; what we know as his 'passion'. They did so and in the four gospels included, without embellishment of detail to harmonise each account with the others, what they knew to be true.

By the end of the day that we know as Easter Sunday, and on days following, they experienced his rising from the tomb and they needed to tell and re-tell the events that had led up to it by means of recounting the events of what we now call 'Holy Week.'

The events

The route from the Temple Mount to the Kidron Valley involves a descent of some three hundred feet or so. Nowadays a busy road parallels the route of the Kidron river, perhaps better described as a wadi due to its intermittent flow. Having crossed it Jesus and the disciples enter a 'garden'. This is at the foot of the Mount of Olives. The location is given by Matthew and Mark as 'Gethsemane', and by Luke as the 'Mount of Olives'.

Judas Iscariot arrived with a detachment of Roman military and police, again a difference in detail from the other three gospels (the 'synoptic' gospels) where a 'crowd' came along to take Jesus. Explaining this disparity could well take us into detailed discussion well beyond the scope of this little devotional book. But there is one alluring thought that could lie behind John's inclusion of Roman authorities in the arrest of Jesus. Namely, that he was underlining the culpability of both Gentiles and Jews in the capture of Jesus along with betrayal by one of his closest followers. By this means no one, whether an individual or a grouping, escapes responsibility for the death of Jesus. This is so whether those concerned were the actual executioners, the prosecutors or any other who had a part to play in the drama of Jesus' arrest and death by what they did, great or small, direct or incidental.

Judas and the arresting cohort arrived whilst it was night. The same night in which Judas had left the meal table to seek out those who would accompany him to the garden where Jesus regularly went. From John 18:2, "Now Judas . . . also knew the place, because Jesus often met there with his disciples".

What is supremely evident in the way that John portrays Jesus is the self-control that Jesus shows throughout the scene as well as control over the unfolding events.

When Jesus asks the soldiers and the police who they are looking for he confirms that he is "Jesus of Nazareth". This doesn't happen once, but twice. At the second time of confirming that it was he whom they were looking for Jesus says to the guard that they should let "these men", namely the disciples, go. This stands as an indication of his preparedness to be sacrificed on behalf of, and in the place of, others.[4]

There is an incongruity, I suggest, between the arresting cohort falling down in front of Jesus when he announces who he is with their intention to arrest him, and then them actually doing so.

Officials charged with the task of arresting someone do not normally fall down before the one they are to arrest. One could conjecture that they were caught by an involuntary motor reaction to the divine presence before them. Whilst such a reaction is well attested in Christian revivalist circles it would not be expected in a circumstance like this; most especially when they then go on to fulfil their duty by arresting the one before whom they have, barely minutes earlier, been prostrate.

The verb that John uses in his gospel to signify the cohort's 'falling' before Jesus is *pipto*. This is not a word that one would expect in a religious context. It simply means that they 'fell down' most likely having stepped back. However, the fact that Jesus uses the self-description 'I am' in this location, and does so twice, fits a wider theological motif in John's gospel. Here is what I mean by this. At a number of points in John's gospel Jesus speaks of himself in terms of 'I am'. Thus, for example: "I am he" [i.e. the Messiah](4:26), "I am the bread of life" (6:35), "I am the living bread" (6:51), "I am the light of the world" (8:12), "I am the gate" (10:9), "I am the resurrection and the life" (11:25), "I am the way the truth and the life" (14:6), "I am the true vine" (15:1).

In each of these self-descriptions Jesus adds teaching to illustrate what he means by the 'I am' saying. By contrast, however, in the garden, moments before his arrest, no teaching follows the twofold admission "I am he". What does follow, as we have seen, is much more emphatically and dramatically descriptive than any words could capture. Namely that the cohort of soldiers and police fall to the ground before Jesus. It is almost as if John, as the narrator of this gospel account, is providing for his readers an 'action', a truly dramatic event, on the part of those before Jesus as the performative explanation of what he meant.

What I mean by this is that even though they have come to arrest him, and then actually do so, his divinity, who he is, is attested by their involuntary collapse to the ground. In such a context as this Jesus does not need to give

---

4 We note that other gospels have Jesus' identity being given away by Judas as he kissed him (Matthew and Mark; Luke, however, indicates Judas' intention to kiss Jesus but does not record him actually doing so).

any teaching to explain here what he means by the 'I am' statement. The physiological collapse of his captors says all that needs to be said.

To extend this interpretation to the level of metaphor one could read this story of the soldiers and police officers falling down before Jesus as a portrayal of the way that all authorities should react when in the presence of the Lord.

Craig Keener recognises there is no historical corroboration for what happened to the arresting force though he does note other instances of involuntary physiological collapse in given circumstances of religious experience.[5] My own view here is that it matters not whether or not there is any historical corroboration. What is happening here is that the author of John's gospel is making a theological point about the divinity of Jesus as the Messiah. His meaning is that powers of darkness, represented here by Judas Iscariot and the arresting cohort (noting again that this drama takes place when "it is night") cannot 'stand' before the presence of God even though they then go on to do that which Jesus freely wills should be done.

In other words, John's point here is theological, regardless of whether or not it is historical.

Peter's assault on Malchus: John's Gospel and Mark's Gospel

Contributing to the turbulence of events in the garden is Peter's assault on Malchus. One blow from Peter's sword removed Malchus' ear, we are told. How this happened we cannot tell. If the result was as intended, then Peter's accuracy is astonishing. For ear removal such as this to be accomplished, and in this manner, then Malchus would have needed to have remained very still. If his ear was not the intended target then we might well assume that Peter was aiming for Malchus' neck, or head, or possibly his upper thorax. Seeking to dodge the sword strike, the hapless Malchus duly lost his ear in doing so. Further conjecture at this point and on this point need detain us no further for we can look deeper into the narrative than simple surface details allow.

In the garden scene Jesus is the one whom we have presented as supremely in control of himself, of the events, and of all those before him. Peter, meanwhile, who has not long before challenged Jesus for washing his feet now seeks to assert his own individual authority and command once more and does so with his sword. Again, Peter gets it wrong. For, as Jesus rebuked him at the meal table for refusing to have his feet washed, once more Jesus rebukes Peter, "Put your sword back into its sheath". (18:11)

---

5 Keener, *The Gospel of John*, 1081-82.

Jesus says this quite deliberately for he has to go the way that God the Father requires him to go. Jesus is accepting his fate even if Peter, as one of the disciples, is not able to do so without protest. Jesus' rhetorical words, in the same place, are, "Am I not to drink the cup that the Father has given me?" Yet again, we can see John's portrait of Jesus as someone in complete control of everything, perhaps most noticeably his emotions.

Once more John's narrative picture of Jesus stands in significant contrast to the distressed and agitated Jesus that is portrayed in Mark's Gospel. In Mark 14:32ff. Jesus prays for the "hour to pass from him" (14:35) and for the "cup to be removed from him" (14:36, adapted). In Mark, Jesus accepts and resigns himself to the will of the Father. By doing so, Jesus' prayer in Gethsemane in Mark's Gospel is not answered in the way that Jesus wanted, but rather, that by aligning himself in prayer to God's will the world got what it needed in the sacrifice of Jesus.

In this sense at least therefore, the gospels of Mark and John are speaking of the same thing although are doing so from differing vantage points. Both are testifying to the willingness of Jesus to live out the will of God. Mark portrays Jesus doing so out of a prelude of distress. John does so figuring Jesus as one in complete control. Each writer in his own way is presenting us with a facet of who Jesus is; fully human and fully divine. To understand who Jesus is one needs both facets. The one without the other would miss the truth that the other was giving. Both authors are theological in their presentation of the historical and personal testimony available to each, and as each witnessed it.

And so to today

In my time as the University Chaplain to the University of Dundee in eastern Scotland an up-and-coming artist called Nael Hanna presented an exhibition of his artwork in the University's Chapel. It was a fine exhibition and displayed the early talent of someone who has proved to be one of Scotland's most original contemporary painters.

Hanna is an Iraqi Christian, and if my memory serves me correctly, his family originates from Mosul. The work in this exhibition displayed his Christian roots with, unsurprisingly given his origins, much of it being very dark. One painting, a large oil set in landscape frame, had many, many faces and features in torment and anxiety. Closer gazing at the painting released to the viewer many crosses set into the overall work. These were quite explicitly images of the cross that Christian faith associates with the death of Jesus. They were there at every touch and turn of this painting of suffering.

That image has stayed with me since those days in the 1980s when we hosted that exhibition for Hanna; namely that the cross which testifies to Christ's suffering is there at every point and from every angle of human suffering. Where there is human distress so the cross of Christ can be found.

Whether it be in the suffering of those refugees fleeing from their homes in countries ravaged by conflict and war; whether in communities flooded out by winter rains, or in the suffering of those punished by unemployment, whether in the confusion of those de-personalised by loss of self-worth or meaning, or whether in those racked by unrelenting illness or whether in others coming to terms with bereavement. Wherever there is suffering there the cross is to be found.

The suffering Christ entered our suffering so that when we have to face trials and difficulties (of whatever form) we know that God has faced it in the person of Jesus, and still does so. In the midst of the darkness of Good Friday Jesus looks down from the cross and to some he says, "This day you will be with me in paradise". To others he says "Son, behold your mother", and to mothers he says, "Mother, behold your son". In the cross, on the cross, Jesus recognises us all and through the cross to everyone he says, "It is accomplished".

However, something before us must now be considered. For this to come about I will do two things in my next chapter. I will complete the story of Jesus' death and of his dying as he is laid in his tomb towards the close of that first Good Friday and as the Jewish Sabbath observance was soon to begin. Second, I will then seek to contemplate the silence of Holy Saturday. Nothing is said of this in the Gospels. Jesus was dead and was buried on the Friday. Saturday is passed over in all the gospels in silence. The next we hear in the passion story of Jesus is of Mary of Magdala going to his grave early on the third day after he died.

What we must ask is the significance of the silence in the gospels as Jesus lay dead, and before he rose from that death.

A meditation from music

My suggestion for a reflection from the world of music is enigmatic. Enigmatic in that I cannot trace, much as I and others assisting me have searched, for a copy of its lyrics. Equally, repeated listening to the song on

YouTube does not reveal much clarity in the words being sung beyond the first few stanzas.

The melody begins with a piano arpeggio that introduces backing voices initially held very much in the background. A first soloist arrives to set the scene. But as a second soloist develops the song discernment of specific lyrics become increasingly difficult, except for a few snatches along the way, and not least because the backing voices become more prominent.[6]

I have stuck with this song, however, thinking that perhaps this is how things should be for a Good Friday meditation. Namely that as the events of that fateful day proceeded towards and through the death of Jesus perhaps nothing should be clear. The rhythmic tumbling of fusing voices, enfolded within a blues harmony of gathering drama, can together say all that needs to be said for one to move into prayerful reflection. Here then are the opening lines from the Pilgrim Travellers song, *How Jesus Died* and some indication of the other themes which the song involves. I invite the reader to listen to the song online. The following lyrics are approximated to the song:

For, if I die and my soul be lost
It's nobody's fault but mine.

Oh, I want to tell you a story
That we all should believe
How Jesus died for you and for me.

Oh, and Isaac spoke of the coming of a sign
Just before He left His home on high.

And let me use gospels that heard a man crying,
"Jesus is born and He surely must die."

And let me tell you just how He died;
For just a little silver He was crucified

Let me tell you just why he died;
By his friend Peter He was denied . . .

Remaining lyrics not available but remaining themes in the song include Judas' *betrayal, Pilate's hand-washing, the 6th to 9th hour and mother Mary crying.*

---

6 I am grateful to my son, Timothy Gillies, for help in understanding and rendering this account of the Pilgrim Travellers song.

Chapter Seven
HOLY SATURDAY (EASTER EVE)
Jesus has died

A Prayer
O God,
creator of heaven and earth:
as the crucified body of your dear Son was laid in the tomb,
and rested on this holy Sabbath;
so may we await with him the coming of the third day,
and rise with him to newness of life;
through Jesus Christ our Lord,
who now lives and reigns with you,
in the unity of the Holy Spirit,
one God, world without end.
Amen

John 19:38-42
The Burial of Jesus
38 [38]After these things, Joseph of Arimathea, who was a disciple
of Jesus, though a secret one because of his fear of the Jews, asked
Pilate to let him take away the body of Jesus. Pilate gave him
permission; so he came and removed his body. [39]Nicodemus, who
had at first come to Jesus by night, also came, bringing a mixture
of myrrh and aloes, weighing about a hundred pounds. [40]They took
the body of Jesus and wrapped it with the spices in linen cloths,
according to the burial custom of the Jews.[41]Now there was a garden
in the place where he was crucified, and in the garden there was a
new tomb in which no one had ever been laid. [42]And so, because it
was the Jewish day of Preparation, and the tomb was nearby, they
laid Jesus there.[1]

---

1 Alternative Reading set for Daily Eucharist, Holy Saturday (Easter Eve), Years A,
B and C.

Introduction

The biblical passage given in the lection of readings from John's Gospel for Holy Saturday, Easter Eve, is the narrative of Joseph of Arimathea and Nicodemus seeking permission to take the body of Jesus. Their desire was to anoint the body prior to burial and then see to the burial itself. I look at this first. What is taking place is the entombment, the entombing, of Jesus. John's gospel records that Joseph of Arimathea and Nicodemus are our two principal named characters in this action.

Next, the entombment of Jesus also refers to that period of time between the dead Jesus being laid in his grave (and the tomb sealed with the large circular stone disc cover) up to and including his bodily resurrection. There are no witnesses to what happened in Jesus' grave during this period.

In what follows I will reflect on the Gospel account of Joseph of Arimathea and Nicodemus taking and anointing the body of Jesus and also to that period of time when Jesus lay in the tomb, prior to his rising, and of what the entombment might mean in this context.

The Setting

The narrative begins in the precincts of Pilate's place of authority as Joseph of Arimathea approaches the Roman Governor to ask for the body of Jesus so that it can be anointed, prepared for burial and then carried for the burial to take place before the Sabbath begins. He, with another Jewish leader, Nicodemus must act in haste. Silent in the narrative are those who, as we shall see, would have assisted these two Jewish leaders in their devotion to the duty of burial, and in their respect for Jesus.

Absent also in any Gospel is an account of Jesus' actual rising from the dead.

Joseph of Arimathea and Nicodemus

The descriptions given in John's Gospel of Joseph of Arimathea[2] and Nicodemus are at one and the same time intriguing and contrasting. Joseph of Arimathea is described by John as a 'secret disciple'. The reason for this is given as his fear of the Jews. John 12:42, for example, and referring to others like Joseph of Arimathea, reads, ". . . many, even of the authorities, believed

2 Arimathea, identified by Eusebius as a short distance north west of Jerusalem.

in him. But because of the Pharisees they did not confess it, for fear that they would be put out of the synagogue . . ."

After the death of Jesus, in point of fact, very close to the death of Jesus, Joseph of Arimathea sought audience with Pilate so that he might take the body of Jesus for appropriate burial. Joseph of Arimathea's approach to Pilate to secure the body of Jesus is attested in all four gospels.[3] He was joined by another Jewish leader, Nicodemus.

Nicodemus was a Pharisee and is described as a "leader of the Jews". Interestingly, he had previously sought out Jesus and had "come to him by night". Their encounter is given in John 3. His conversation with Jesus, at night, is seen as a discreet, seemingly covert, action. In another location, John 7, Nicodemus had in his professional sphere, previously, spoken on behalf of Jesus, and the need for a fair trial were he to be arrested. Nicodemus' colleagues, the passage suggests, were seeking to have Jesus arrested and brought to them by means far less than those required by the law. Nicodemus saw this was wrong. Jesus, like all others, deserved justice.

By seeking to anoint Jesus' body for burial, and then to carry out the burial themselves, these two men, who had previously kept their acknowledgment of Jesus discreet, now renounce this previous 'secrecy'. The sheer volume of spices that Nicodemus brought for them to use for the anointing is lavish in the extreme. The pattern that they followed echoes detail given in 2 Chronicles 16:14.[4] Ruth Edwards concludes, "Nicodemus is a good man doing Jesus a service".[5]

It would be wrong to think that Joseph of Arimathea and Nicodemus buried Jesus on their own. Bauckham and Hart have computed the weight of the spices to be half a hundredweight and to be of vast expense. Craig Keener estimates the weight to be slightly more than that, namely seventy-five pounds. It is true that the weight of spices was great, but whether Bauckham and Hart's further claim that Nicodemus would have had "a whole procession of servants carrying the spices"[6] is also true or imaginative hyperbole we cannot say. Three or four fit people could carry the load. However more than the two men, the

---

3 Cf. Luke 23:50f., Mark 15:43, and Matthew 27:57.

4 Josephus in *Jewish Antiquities* (Book 17: 8.3, para 199) recounts the lavish use of spices for a person considered of great honour. In this case it was Archelaus burying his father Herod, and doing so with significant pomp and ceremony.

5 Ruth B. Edwards, *Discovering John*, SPCK, 2014, 123.

6 Richard Bauckham and Trevor Hart, with illustrations by Helen Firth, *At the Cross*, Darton, Longman and Todd, London 1999, 107.

secret disciple and the disciple who came by night, would have been needed to lift and move Jesus' body and, of course, the large number of spices as well. Given their position in leadership, servants or assistants would be available. Because of the short time before the start of the Sabbath what had to be done needed to be done quickly and would indeed need more staffing than just Joseph of Arimathea and Nicodemus on their own.

Certainly, and given the volume of spices brought to Jesus for his burial anointing, the cost of these unguents would be vast. It is interesting to note an echo between the gifts brought to Jesus, which included spices, by (presumably) Gentile rulers from the east at his birth with this gift of spices by Jewish leaders at his death.

Nicodemus was a man of power and influence and that for someone in his position to regard Jesus in the way he did is very significant. Pilate had had placed over Jesus on the cross the inscription, "The King of the Jews". Nicodemus and Joseph of Arimathea were taking this title literally and by burying Jesus in the way they did they were burying, as they saw it, a king.[7]

Clearly these two previously discreet allies of Jesus believed that in burial he deserved respect, even if in his trial and summary execution Jesus had been denied that. Craig Keener notes whilst Jesus' other followers, those with whom he had shared his last supper, had deserted him these two did not. Jesus' disciples where nowhere to be seen. By contrast, the previously secret disciples, Joseph of Arimathea and Nicodemus now left discretion behind and attended openly to Jesus in death and did so during daylight hours.

They were prepared to give honour to God, even in this seemingly final hour and to put duty to the dead man, Jesus, before their own previously preferred well-being and standing.[8]

What these two hitherto discreet and secretive disciples did in the burial of Jesus is a testimony of their, now open, devotion to him. We cannot classify their devotion as faith based on the resurrection, for that had yet to take place. But we can consider it to be at the level of deep respect and of highest regard.

Their actions may be considered typologically. By being secretive, previously, they have now come out into the open. And again, by coming to Jesus in darkness earlier on in John's narrative, when it was night, Nicodemus, with Joseph of Arimathea, now prepares the body of Jesus for burial in full

---

7 Craig Keener in *The Gospel of John: A Commentary*, vol. 2, Hendrickson Publishers, Peabody, Massachusetts 2003, notes other lavish burials, 1163-64.
8 Keener, *op. cit.*, 1157.

view for all to see. The motif of moving from darkness to light is strong in John's gospel and can also be recognised as a metaphor for those who, leaving a previous dark or hidden life behind, now live in the open light of faith.

The tomb of Jesus

Jewish prohibition of the Roman preference for allowing corpses to remain on their crucifixion crosses would however give some succour to these two men who were doing what they considered to be their duty to do. Deuteronomic law[9] would also be their aid in seeking to secure decent burial for Jesus. Hemer cites Deuteronomy 21:22-23 when he writes that ". . . a hanged man on a tree shall not remain all night there, but be buried the same day, that the land be not defiled, for he is accursed."[10]

Perhaps we might conjecture that the Jewish authorities would be relieved that these two, whatever other intention they had, visibly followed the prescriptions of the law, and thus were seen to be acting on behalf of the other Jewish authorities, by doing that which they knew needed to be done according to the precepts of their law.

Meantime Pilate, having previously washed his hands of Jesus' disposal in life, seemingly imposed no condition upon his burial. In all likelihood Pilate simply wanted rid of the body of Jesus and desired to court no further bother from the Jewish authorities on account of this troublesome Jewish criminal. Nor would he seek the punishment of Joseph of Arimathea on grounds of association with Jesus arising from his request for the body. Pilate simply wanted the affair over and past. Refusal to grant burial in the Jewish tradition might create more fuss than he thought the dead Jesus was worth.

Accordingly, the tradition behind all four gospels and supported in Paul's writings in his Letters both to the Romans and Corinthians leads us to the conclusion that the burial of Jesus was, as Keener puts it, in an "honorable, distinguishable grave"[11] without either Roman or Jewish inhibition.

---

9 Keener cites Deuteronomy 21:23, and see also Josephus, *The Jewish War* 4:317 in this regard, ". . . the Jews pay so much regard to obsequies that even those found guilty and crucified are taken down and buried before sunset." It was the day of preparation when everyone would be getting ready and having everything in place, on time, for the Passover festival to begin.

10 C.J. Hemer, 'Bury', in *The New International Dictionary of New Testament Theology*, vol. 1, Paternoster Press, Carlisle 1996, 265.

11 Keener, *op. cit.*, 1158.

The use of linen strips, or a shroud, to bind the body fits the pattern of Jewish burials at that time. Spices, both to quench the smell of a rotting body, and to pay tribute similarly accord with Jewish practice. The text of John 19:40 suggests that the spices were placed between the wrappings, or layers, of Jesus' grave clothes.

At no place in the narrative of Jesus being prepared for burial, or during the act of his burial, is there any indication that those who were doing these things, nor yet John in recounting the particular events in his gospel, considered that Jesus was to rise from the dead. Brown comments, "Contemporary Judaism had no concept of a dying and rising Messiah."[12]

The place of Jesus' burial, a new, in the sense of previously unused, family grave owned by Joseph of Arimathea, as attested in Matthew 27:60, was near to the site of the crucifixion and not beyond the city in any location reserved for criminals. Because the grave would have been visited from very early after the crucifixion and, in all certainty, continually from then onwards its location is very likely to be where it is now given to be, namely in, or perhaps better, under, the Church of the Holy Sepulchre in Jerusalem. The location has been attested from very earliest times.[13] The Venerable Bede in the eighth century reported what came to him from a pilgrim to Jerusalem in his homily on Mark's Gospel:

> It was a vaulted chamber, hollowed out of rock. Its height was such that a person standing in the middle could touch the summit with his hand. Its entrance faced east, and the great stone about which the gospel tells us was placed over it. To the right as one enters was the place that was specially prepared as a resting place for the Lord's body, seven feet in length, about two feet above the rest of the floor. The opening was not made like that of ordinary sepulchres, from above, but entirely from the side, from which the body could be placed inside.

Family burial plots in this part of Jerusalem, "would often have been caves covered by a large stone rolled in a groove."[14] Impossible to move from within, they would have been heavy and difficult to move from outside.

---

12 C. Brown, 'Resurrection' in *The New International Dictionary op. cit.*, vol. 3, 296.
13 See Charles H. Talbert, *Reading John*, SPCK, London 1992, 246 and Keener, *op. cit.*, 1166, notes 867 and 868 refer. I am also indebted to Keener for pointing me to the quotation from the Venerable Bede. I quote Keener's citation of it.
14 Keener, *op. cit.*, 1165.

What happened in the grave?

None of the scriptures portray what happened at the resurrection. There were no witnesses to it happening. On the actual event of Jesus rising from death there is no narrative.

Elsewhere narrative testimony of the rising of Jesus is given. In the Gospel of Peter, a non-canonical, or apocryphal Gospel, such an account exists. It dates from somewhere between AD70 and 160. Though similar in some respects to the four canonical Gospels, in significant and other respects (for example its exoneration of Pilate and vilification of the Jews, that Jesus felt no pain in his dying if, according to this gospel, he did indeed die) it differs and diverges markedly.

In the Gospel of Peter dramatic and picturesque narrative portrays the rising of Jesus and of the stone's capacity to roll away from the entrance of the tomb without human intervention. The Gospel of Peter has nothing of the starkness of the four canonical gospels and may be taken as a poetic account that provides an imaginative and created narrative of that for which there is no witnessed narrative.

In the world of art, through the centuries, there is much imaginative play on canvas and on board with the resurrection of Jesus. In many works of art Jesus is shown stepping out of his tomb in bodily form very often carrying what is best described as a 'St George's flag'; a red cross against a white background, this being a traditional symbol of Jesus' resurrection.

Artistic representations of the rising of Jesus work at different cognitive, aesthetic and affective levels from that of the written text. No one would reasonably assume that a painting of Jesus' departing from his tomb equated with what a photographer might have captured with camera and lens had such been possible at the moment Jesus emerged. And nor should we take non-canonical texts (such as the Gospel of Peter) with their figurative detail of the rising of Jesus as any more accurate than, let us say, a Renaissance altar triptych of the same event. Each in their own way seeks to portray an event about which the Gospels themselves remain silent.

Music similarly, through its own special medium of aesthetic communication, works with ranging levels of appreciation and understanding. One musician, Krzysztof Penderecki, has explored the theme before us in this chapter. Penderecki has become established as a significant Polish orchestral and choral composer and conductor in the modern genres of polyphony and discord. His birth in 1933, his subsequent graduation in music at the Superior School in Krakow together with his subsequent lifetime commitment to music encompassed the nationalism of pre-war Poland, the Nazi overthrow of his country and its post-war Stalinisation (if I may be permitted that shorthand descriptor). The haunting tones of his compositions variously image and reflect dark shadows and piercing shards from each of these difficult periods of his nation's past. At the same time, Penderecki's music more specifically echoes the tones of traditional Eastern Orthodox liturgy interwoven with modernist experimental sound using voice and instrument. This use of traditional liturgical sound offers more familiar form and content amidst otherwise disturbing dissonance.

I first encountered his *The Entombment of Christ, 1970,* during my seminary years in Edinburgh. In this haunting and difficult work, dedicated to the conductor Eugene Ormandy, Penderecki draws inspiration for this work from the Orthodox liturgy of Holy Saturday. It forms Part One of his large-scale vocal work, *Utrenja* (1970 – 1971). Emma Bragg, a friend and professional musician, and I have talked about Penderecki's *The Entombment of Christ.* In correspondence with me she has described what Penderecki composed:

> [It] focuses on the lamentation of Christ's death as well as the Easter Sunday morning service commemorating the Resurrection. The *Entombment of Christ* is written for three male voices (tenor, bass and 'basso profundo') and two female voices (soprano and mezzo-soprano) all of which are supported by two choirs and orchestra.[15]

It is a disturbing piece to listen to, and though I acknowledge Emma Bragg's further point that the brass and percussion writing is 'particularly rich', more than forty years on from when I first heard it I find it no more pleasing or relaxing now than I did then. Why might this be? For answer we can refer to words from the Apostles Creed where we find the affirmation that Jesus, ". . . was crucified, dead, and buried, *He descended into hell . . .*"[16] These words are all too easily passed over in the familiarity of repetition in congregational recitation. It will be good, therefore, to pause in this reflection and ask the fundamental question, 'What does it mean that Jesus, when dead, went into hell?' What implications surround this?

---

15 With acknowledgment to Emma Bragg for permission to cite this from her letter.
16 From the 'Apostles Creed' in the *Scottish Book of Common Prayer* (emphasis mine).

The silence of the grave

Without wanting to pre-empt what I intend to say in my next chapter let me cite John 19:42 and John 20:1 in strict sequence; they follow one another in John's gospel, "And so, because it was the Jewish day of Preparation, and the tomb was nearby, they laid Jesus there. Early on the first day of the week, while it was still dark, Mary Magdalene came to the tomb . . ."

What is remarkable about these two verses is that absolutely nothing is said about the period of time, a notional thirty-six hours, let us say, after Jesus had been laid out in his grave, dead, and during which period he rose from the dead. This is, at first sight, remarkable. Copious narrative has covered all the events from Jesus arriving at the home of Lazarus, Martha and Mary in Bethany, his arrival in Jerusalem, and all the following events that then led up to his being laid in the tomb.

A significant volume of narrative is also there in John's gospel to cover Jesus' resurrection appearances, initially in Jerusalem and then subsequently in Galilee.

But for the period when Jesus is laid in the tomb there is silence in all four gospels. The gospel writers clearly felt no need to present a story for which there were no witnesses. And yet it is the period when Jesus was in his grave that holds together the two events of, first, his death and, second, his resurrection appearance. If we were to ask the question 'what is it that links the death of Jesus with his rising?' we would have to answer that it is the silence of the tomb.

In the remainder of this Chapter I will consider some of the implications behind this.[17] The modern agenda for this discussion has been set by the prolific writer and theologian Hans Urs von Balthasar in his monumental work *Mysterium Paschale*.[18] Karl Barth also wrote about it in his *Church Dogmatics*.[19] The single most direct volume on the subject in recent

---

17 I considered a related theme in *Three Days in Holy Week*, Handsel Press, 2014, 42-44 in a chapter where my theme was Jesus' cry of derelicition as given in Matthew's gospel.

18 Hans Urs von Balthasar's principal works in this area are *Man in History, Mysterium Paschale, The Glory of the Lord* (vol. 7), *Theology: The New Covenant*. All cited from Lewis, below, 2 n.1. Lewis also notes Gregory of Nyssa as alone "perceiving much dogmatic significance in Holy Saturday".

19 Karl Barth eds. G.W. Bromiley and T.F. Torrance, *Church Dogmatics*, vol. 4:1 and vol. 4:2 particularly, T&T Clark, Edinburgh 1958.

times is the heroic work of theology and spirituality *Between Cross and Resurrection* by Alan Lewis.[20]

The silence that is Holy Saturday

Alan Lewis invites his readers to consider what Holy Saturday was like for those followers of Jesus who had experienced his life, heard his teaching, and only hours before had become bereaved at his death. They did not know what we, with hindsight, know. Namely that Jesus would rise from the dead. We know that Jesus' *post mortem* experience lasted from late on what we know as Good Friday to early on the first Easter Sunday. Those at the time could not to know this.

If, again to follow Lewis, we imagine ourselves standing where they stood on that dark Saturday of death and looked back what would they have thought of Jesus' life? Without knowing that he was to rise within the next day or so they would have seen a life of promise. A life of kingdom teaching, miracle working, exorcisms, and the application of their ancient Law, with so much more, presented a new way. However, they would have seen his direct challenge to the Jerusalem Temple authorities fail, for Jesus did nothing to retract what he had said or to defend himself in such a way as to navigate a course away from his capital punishment sentence. They would have seen him similarly fail before Pilate. And on the cross they would have heard his cry that God had forsaken him.

On that Saturday this is where they would have been. Jesus had gone, was dead and buried. All they had hoped for under his teaching from God was lost and ended. The divine promise of a kingdom, yet to come, had come to nothing. God had forsaken them.

From the same perspective, what would these followers have seen had they cast their eyes forward. There would have been no future. In their bereaved loss of divine promise and expectation they could not know of Jesus' more or less imminent resurrection. An empty future lay ahead. They too could have cried the same anguished death cry of Jesus, 'My God, my God, why have you forsaken me [us]?'

---

20 Alan E. Lewis, *Between Cross and Resurrection: A Theology of Holy Saturday*, Eerdmans, Grand Rapids, Michigan 2003. 'Heroic' because Lewis had a terminal cancer diagnosed during the course of his work on this book. Accordingly his own life became a very personal testament to the volume he was preparing for publication.

In the modern collection of Psalms as used by the Scottish Episcopal Church a short prayer is added to end each one. The particular prayer given at the end of Psalm 22 (which has the original words for Jesus' cry of dereliction from the cross) begins, "Father, your tortured Son felt abandoned . . ." The word 'felt' here is a typical twentieth and twenty-first century attempt to sugar the bitter pill of Jesus' real death; and to coat what was actually happening to him with a saccharine veneer that says he only *felt* he was abandoned by God. It is too much to ask of super-sensitive, avoid-pain-at-all-costs contemporary western humanity, to take on board the reality that Jesus was actually dying and that in his death God was indeed abandoning him to a totally human, truly real death. And into that place of hell where God was not, Jesus was going, and indeed, went. It was real.

Faced with the actual fact of the death of Jesus, there was for his followers the consequent loss and death of all that faith had held for them in and through his life. In his death, all that had gone. In their gaze towards the future, there was now no future.

That Mary of Magdala came to the grave in the way she did, and for the purpose that led her to it, she too believed that Jesus' death confirmed all that the authorities considered true about him. He was no more. His grave was the proof of God's abandonment of him. On that Holy Saturday with only the recollection of what had been, with the failure of it all, and with no prospect ahead, she could think no other.

And yet, in loving duty and service to the decaying cadaver of Jesus Mary of Magdala was to tread her way to his grave early the next morning. Not for her today's twenty-first century discreet despatch and disposal of the dead body of a loved one thereby freeing those left behind to party and celebrate the life now ended. The dead surely deserve better, by way of mourning respect, than modernising trends seem to offer.

We can say, as has just been hinted, that the grave was, on that first Holy Saturday, the Temple and occupying authorities' confirmation from their perspectives that all that Jesus had advocated and lived for was now negated, lost and gone. He could have saved himself but did not. From their perspective on that Holy Saturday a good job had been done. All that they had needed to do was concluded. It was finished; everything accomplished.

However, from the perspective of God's redemption of all things there is more that needs to be said. For God to be God his human frame had to encompass everything from pre-existence with the Father and the Spirit, onwards successively to his human birth, his human death and onwards to resurrection, and thence to ascension and eternal union with the Father and the Spirit.

But finally, what of Jesus in the grave? He had been laid there; the stone rolled into place; and in the aloneness and darkness his body would be beginning its decay. Jesus was laid where the dead are. His death took him to the place of the dead. Somehow, we know not how or when, this putrefying corpse left the place of the dead and rose to new life. We know not whether this resurrection of Jesus was instantaneous or whether it took place over a period of time, and if the latter then we know not its duration.

Either way the resurrection happened in time and within our understanding of time's temporal flow. It was an event in time that linked the historical event of the crucifixion with the historical event of the body's resurrection. And it was this link that each of the Gospel writers passes over in silence.

If Jesus had not fully died God could not raise him from the dead. God could only overcome death if there had been a real death. God could only reverse (if that is the correct word) through resurrection from death, the abandonment of Jesus in Good Friday's death if it had actually happened. The dying and death of Jesus took place in real time. So too did his resurrection. The connecting link between Good Friday death and Easter Sunday rising is there in the mystery that is the Jerusalem tomb of Holy Saturday.

In Conclusion

I finish with words of G.E. Ladd, quoted by Brown:

[the resurrection] was an event that was observed by no one, an event caused by God – indeed, an event in which the world of God intersected the world of time and space . . . All that the historian as such can say is that something marvellous has happened here. *Only those who have reason to believe in the God to whom the Bible witnesses can accept the witness of the gospels, viz., that God raised Jesus from the dead.*[21]

---

21   Cited from Brown, 'Resurrection', *op. cit.*, 297.

Chapter Eight

EASTER SUNDAY

In the garden

A Prayer
Almighty God,
who, through your Son, Jesus Christ,
has overcome death and opened the gates of eternal life:
grant that we, who celebrate with joy the day of his resurrection,
may be raised from the death of sin by your life-giving Spirit;
through the same Jesus Christ, our Lord,
who lives and reigns with you,
in the unity of the Holy Spirit,
one God, world without end.
Amen

John 20:1-18
The Resurrection of Jesus
[1]Early on the first day of the week, while it was still dark, Mary Magdalene came to the tomb and saw that the stone had been removed from the tomb. [2]So she ran and went to Simon Peter and the other disciple, the one whom Jesus loved, and said to them, 'They have taken the Lord out of the tomb, and we do not know where they have laid him.' [3]Then Peter and the other disciple set out and went towards the tomb. [4]The two were running together, but the other disciple outran Peter and reached the tomb first. [5]He bent down to look in and saw the linen wrappings lying there, but he did not go in. [6]Then Simon Peter came, following him, and went into the tomb. He saw the linen wrappings lying there, [7]and the cloth that had been on Jesus' head, not lying with the linen wrappings but rolled up in a place by itself. [8]Then the other disciple, who reached the tomb first, also went in, and he saw and believed; [9]for as yet they did not understand the scripture, that he must rise from the dead. [10]Then the disciples returned to their homes.

Jesus Appears to Mary Magdalene

[11]But Mary stood weeping outside the tomb. As she wept, she bent over to look into the tomb; [12]and she saw two angels in white, sitting where the body of Jesus had been lying, one at the head and the other at the feet. [13]They said to her, "Woman, why are you weeping?" She said to them, "They have taken away my Lord, and I do not know where they have laid him." [14]When she had said this, she turned around and saw Jesus standing there, but she did not know that it was Jesus. [15]Jesus said to her, "Woman, why are you weeping? Whom are you looking for?" Supposing him to be the gardener, she said to him, "Sir, if you have carried him away, tell me where you have laid him, and I will take him away." [16]Jesus said to her, "Mary!" She turned and said to him in Hebrew, "Rabbouni!" (which means Teacher). [17]Jesus said to her, "Do not hold on to me, because I have not yet ascended to the Father. But go to my brothers and say to them, 'I am ascending to my Father and your Father, to my God and your God.'" [18]Mary Magdalene went and announced to the disciples, "I have seen the Lord"; and she told them that he had said these things to her.[1]

---

1 Reading set for Daily Eucharist, Easter Sunday, Year B.

Introduction

"Early on the first day of the week, while it was still dark . . ." are the enticing words that would grace the first sentence of any novel seeking to draw the reader further into what following pages then offer. The time of day is given. The day of the week is announced. And the scene is set in darkness for, two thousand years ago, there would have been only whatever light was around (the moon maybe, tallow candles possibly) for anyone to see by. Against this back-drop we are then told that, "Mary Magdalene came to the tomb . . ." The atmosphere is simultaneously pregnant with anticipation and foreboding.

The Setting

From our vantage point, these two millennia after Mary of Magdala made that early morning walk to the tomb of Jesus, it is hard not to read into these opening words of John 20 the outcome, familiar to all those who already know the Christian story, that Jesus has risen from the tomb. However, though the task may be difficult to visualise from her perspective, it is worthwhile recognising that when Mary of Magdala set off to walk to Jesus' grave she did not know the outcome.

Her full expectation was that Jesus' body would be in its grave where it had been laid on the third day previously in order for it not to remain on the cross of crucifixion during the Jewish Sabbath observance (John 19:42). Her emotion would be racked in bereavement. As darkness betokened the passage of that night so too would her soul be in darkness as she walked towards its end and a coming dawn. The man Jesus had died. He had been executed by crucifixion. Not all that long before she had anointed his feet with hugely expensive perfume.[2] Such was her devotion to him. To her and to those who criticised her extravagance Jesus himself had said that her action was in preparation for his death. That death had now come.

So therefore, to fulfil the requirement to mourn and lament at the graveside for the three days (at which point it was believed that the soul left the putrefying cadaver), she approached the place of Jesus' burial. For Mary of Magdala this would be her duty. For her, also, an act of ongoing devotion.

John's account of the early morning events of that first Easter Sunday significantly resembles in various measures the Gospels of Mark and Matthew,

2 See my chapter above for the Monday of Holy Week.

with the remainder of what John says coming close to Luke's narrative. As we have noted before such discrepancies as there are need not worry or detain us. The authors and writers of the Gospels wrote what they knew of the events that happened. Their concern was not the forensic harmonisation of their material, and Craig Keener notes the "liberties literary historians [at that time] sometimes applied on details".[3] Each spoke of the truth, and as a whole together they testify to it.

It is also fair to say that even the most liberally sceptical of modern day interpreters acknowledge that the very earliest disciples (and their successors for centuries to come including today) believed that Jesus had risen bodily from the tomb. I also stand in that ancient tradition.

The drama unfolds

Arriving at the tomb of Jesus Mary of Magdala finds that the stone disc which had been placed at the front of the grave had been rolled away. In the darkness of that early morning we can conjecture how she might have made that discovery. Had she been carrying a burning torch to help her see where to walk? How close was she when she found the stone rolled to one side? If she was carrying a lighted torch, as we might surmise she was, did the flickering flame cast confusing shadows as she sought to apprehend the unexpected find that was before her. Fearing the worst, that the body of Jesus had been taken away, Mary of Magdala reports that, "They have taken the Lord out of the tomb" and adds that, "we do not know where they have laid him".

At this point it is necessary to note that the text of John's Gospel does not tell us who 'they' are. Nor does the gospel say who 'we' are. However, it is conceivable that Mary of Magdala was there with others. Walking there alone would entertain potential risk. If this is so, why are others not mentioned? One can conjecture that John, knowing other accounts circulating in the very earliest Christian communities, was aware of a group having made that journey to the tomb and either did not know the others' names or chose to single out Mary of Magdala for specific personal emphasis.[4]

Looking into the tomb of Jesus she found it to be empty and ran immediately, so far as we can tell, to bring this news to Simon Peter and

---

3 Craig Keener, *The Gospel of John: A Commentary,* vol. 2, 1168. Keener also notes other ancient sources, such as of the death of Callisthenes, where different eye witness accounts differ in detail but all advert to the same principal core events.
4 See Keener, *op. cit.,* 1178.

the "other disciple", the one who Jesus loved. Outrunning Simon Peter the beloved disciple arrives first and looks into the tomb, Peter follows and enters the tomb. The narrator of the story in John's Gospel is at pains to outline the arrangement of the various grave clothes within which the (now absent) dead body of Jesus had been laid.

The speed of the action in John's gospel, now being depicted, is dramatic. Despite the rapidity with which these events are being unfolded before us some significant pointers to what has happened to Jesus are being given. The grave clothes, for example.

Robbing of and from graves, though common, was a very serious crime at the time when the New Testament was being written.[5] If thieves had entered the tomb to steal the body (though for what nefarious purpose we cannot tell) their desire would have been for quick escape. Taking time to undress the body, thus to risk being caught, would not have been their desire. They would have taken the body, as it was, grave clothes and all.

Tomb robbers, by contrast, would have been interested in the grave's items of potential value. Namely those spices which the cloths would contain. On this count their interest would have been to leave the undressed body behind and take only whatever spices, and impregnated cloth, as was most valuable to them. As it was the grave clothes remained, lying in the tomb, and the cloth that had been on Jesus' face rolled up and placed by itself. The body is not there. We do not know how, for there were no witnesses to the rising (the resurrection) of Jesus from death. Seemingly, the post-mortem frame of Jesus has passed through those clothes within which it had been wrapped.

The first disciple to arrive at the tomb, the beloved disciple, then entered the tomb after Simon Peter. What he experienced was sufficient for him to believe. He knew, from that moment, that Jesus had risen. It was this human discovery that Jesus was not there which was sufficient for him to come to faith. This was an experience that was, paradoxically we can say, based on the visual absence of Jesus rather than on the incontrovertible fact of his visible presence.

We can read this as a template which betokens coming to faith today. In the visual absence of the physical person Jesus we find him to be truly

---

5 Charles H. Talbert in his commentary, *Reading John,* SPCK, London 1992, writes this, ". . . a decree of the emperor Claudius (41-54 CE), a copy of which was found at Nazareth, orders capital punishment for those destroying tombs, removing bodies, or displacing the sealing stones . . ." 249.

and totally real and at the same time really present. This encounter with the absence of Jesus, both for the beloved disciple, and multitudes like him since – again, myself included - is what makes faith real. It is visual absence that gives rise and occasion to the real presence of Jesus in his risen form.

What is also being foreshadowed in the way the beloved disciple came to believe are the essential elements of Christian faith, namely, personal discovery of the risen reality of Jesus, as was his discovery of the empty tomb and, to follow shortly, witness of this reality to others.

This contrasts with, or maybe we should say, complements, the situation of Mary of Magdala whose perplexity at the empty tomb is highlighted by the fact that she had gone to tell Simon Peter and the beloved disciple that the body has been taken away; removed by human agency she had concluded. It is not so much that she disbelieved that he had risen from the dead when she found the stone rolled aside but rather, in her case, that the moment to come to faith had yet to arrive. The same was then seen to be true of Simon Peter for whom, and though of the two disciples he arrived at the tomb first, the moment to express and verbalise his faith needed more time to form shape. When it did, he was to give threefold affirmation to Jesus and did so in fullest possible contrast to his previous threefold denial of knowing Jesus. This he had done whilst the charcoal crackled and the cock crew with Jesus held in his first hours of captivity.

In spite of the tumultuous events that began with Mary of Magdala finding the stone rolled away right up to the beloved disciple finding belief through encountering the empty tomb, John 20:10 then, somewhat blandly, records the two men 'returning home'! Seemingly as if nothing had happened! What might we make of this?

For Simon Peter the explicit moment of outward faith affirmation was still to come. In his case it would be with a resurrection appearance (see 1 Corinthians 15:5) rather than with the empty tomb. For the beloved disciple, though he believed when he saw the linen clothes in the tomb, John does not record any explicit and outward witness of this. He simply says that the two men, the disciples, went home. A story, though different in kind, may helpfully illustrate something of what might be going on here in the circumstances of these two men.

Some years ago I knew of a man in training for the Roman Catholic priesthood. Whilst in seminary his father died leaving his mother a widow. Because of infirmity and disability she needed 'live in' care at her home. The seminary authorities judged that the son should leave the seminary in order to look after his mother. Accordingly, he returned home to do so.

When in due course, and some years later, the mother died he then re-entered the seminary to complete his training for the priesthood. Through all this his vocation to be a priest was never in doubt. The time, the moment, for him to live that calling in priest's orders had not yet arrived however. Other things were needing to be done. In order for them to be done this young man had to return home. He did so. Obediently.

Mary of Magdala remains by the tomb

All four gospels agree that it was women who went to the tomb of Jesus on that resurrection morning, and all four agree that Mary of Magdala was one of those who did. Interesting it is that in all four accounts the women are named. This is significant for the testimony of women was regarded as inferior to that of men. That the women then sought the male disciples, who in turn verified the women's accounts, is an indication at least of the importance the gospel writers gave to those whose personal experience bore first witness that Jesus had risen from the dead. Proper corroboration was significantly important.

At this precise point in John's narrative there is no indication that Mary of Magdala shared the beloved disciple's belief. It would seem that her grief remained. Again, at this point, something more was needed for her to come to a personal belief in the individual bodily resurrection of Jesus having happened barely hours before, if indeed it was that long.

Mary of Magdala was not only the first person to find the tomb empty, but also, and because she did not leave as had Simon Peter and the beloved disciple, we are told she was the first person to see the risen Jesus. Her desire to remain at the tomb was not so much a result of belief that Jesus had risen so much as her desire to fulfil her duty to, in devotion for, the one who had died and whose body was now gone. In perplexity, there she remained.

Peering into the tomb she sees two angels, one at the head and one at the foot of where Jesus had lain. They tell her not to weep. Out of custom Mary of Magdala would indeed have expressed lamenting grief in an open and probably unrestrained way. We shall see that three times in the verses before us (John 20:11,13,15) she is told not to weep. It was not that her weeping was wrong in itself but rather that it was unnecessary.

John tells us the two angels were dressed in white. A contrast surely with the combined darkness of the night, the deeper gloom of the tomb, and the depth of Mary of Magdala's bereavement. Throughout his Gospel John employs the contrast of light and dark to great rhetorical effect. We need not therefore be surprised that he does so now at this critical moment in his narration of events.

Other than what John tells us, we do not know what the angels looked like, except that they spoke. We do not know their bodily form. All we know is that Mary of Magdala had this experience in her hour of deepest grief and that, perhaps in irony, they asked her why she was weeping. She replied, reprising words from verse 2, "They have taken away my Lord, and I do not know where they have laid him".[6]

Mary of Magdala's statement is a response to the angels who are placed at each end (the head and the foot) of what I might call the 'absence of Jesus body'. The question "Why are you weeping" arose precisely because of this absence. Many people, when grieving through bereavement today, speak of hearing the voice of the one who died, or of hearing a voice which might give a particular message or ask a question of them. To my mind it is pointless to speculate as to whether the angels had or did not have a particular visible form (even though John gives them one) when the main focus of his passage is the question that Mary of Magdala heard.

This, together with her response, powerfully and pictorially sets the scene for what is to follow.

Mary of Magdala with 'The Gardener'

I have deliberately identified 'The Gardener' this way. My reason for doing so will shortly become clear. Upon responding to the angels' question Mary of Magdala turns around. We do not know how she sensed someone was there. She might have heard something. Or simply, as we all do at times, sense the presence of someone close by. The instinctive reaction is to turn and face whoever it might be.

Jesus (though Mary of Magdala does not know it to be him at this point) asks her the same question as did the angels, "Woman, why are you weeping?" Like others in John's Gospel, and also that of Luke, Mary of Magdala is one who it seems does not initially recognise the risen Jesus. He adds the further

---

6 In verse 2 we noted that Mary used the first person plural in her message to the disciples, and also spoke of Jesus as 'the Lord' rather than, as here, 'my Lord'.

question, "Whom are you looking for?" Clearly she is seeking Jesus, though not at this precise moment the living Jesus of faith, but rather the dead body of Jesus so that, in continuation of her devotion, she may retrieve it from wherever it has been (presumably) taken to be deposited, and given decently proper and final burial.

Her immediate assumption is that this figure is the gardener; a quite reasonable assumption given where the scene is taking place. His single-word response is to speak her name: "Mary". At that moment the penny drops, as it were. The disclosure moment of revelation is complete. Mary knows who this 'Gardener' is and she calls him *"Rabbouni"*. In English, 'Teacher'. Uttering this word in encounter with the risen Jesus, the author of John's Gospel speaks of her as 'turning'.

This may seem a curious action, given that she has barely a few seconds previously already turned to face the person behind her. Did she avert her eyes from gazing upon him? This explanation is plausible for many in the scriptures, not least Moses on Mount Sinai, are bidden not to look upon the face of God. But though plausible at one level, this explanation is unlikely because Jesus bids her not to hold onto him. She could not do so with ease if she had turned her back towards him.[7]

Might it be that the author of John's gospel had simply forgotten what he had previously said concerning Mary of Magdala turning around? Or that he was deliberately repeating himself. The former is unlikely given the sophistication of John's Gospel text. Such an error is inconceivable. Likewise, and on the second point, John would not repeat himself so clumsily.

More probably, I venture to suggest, is the thought that 'turning' as given here in John 20:16 refers to the change in life that comes about with commitment in and to faith in the risen Jesus. Though personally I have never been anything other than a fully believing Christian, I do know that when there is a genuine and true conversion to Christian faith one's life is 'turned around'. I have seen it happen.

---

7 Harold W. Attridge's article "Don't be touching me: Recent Feminist Scholarship on Mary Magdalene" in Amy-Jill Levine, *A Feminist Companion to John* (two volumes), Sheffield Academic Press, Sheffield 2002, offers an assessment of a number of feminist readings of the encounter between Jesus and Mary Magdalene. His overview helpfully provides a useful examination of the topic for those who might want to explore feminist biblical scholarship in this area. What he writes offers an approach from a perspective different from my own.

Equally, and in the same vein, Jesus tells Mary of Magdala not to hold on to him, or perhaps better, 'stop holding on to [him]'. This last reading of the text fits better with what Mary of Magdala has come to do at the graveside, namely to lament in grief by the body of the dead Jesus. She is now commanded to hold on to him (be that physical or emotional) *no longer*. What was once physical must now be let go. A new era has dawned. Having overcome death and the restriction of the tomb Jesus must now return ('ascend') to the Father.

But what of 'The Gardener'? Obviously, we know from the literal text that this was not an encounter with the cemetery gardener. Perhaps, just perhaps, there is a way of reading this passage such that we can say that Mary of Magdala did indeed meet 'The Gardener'.[8] What do I mean by this?

From the perspective of the twenty-first century we have the advantage of hindsight and overview. We know the outcome of Jesus' crucifixion, namely that he rose from death. Resurrection was the consequence of his crucifixion. We have the advantage of a systematically ordered theology which articulates the way, or ways, by which Jesus' death overcame all limitations of finitude and put human frailty, in its sinfulness and incompletion, right with God. We know also, through the pictorial testimony of the Old Testament that it was human disobedience that got things wrong with God in the first place. What's more, we know that this didn't just happen once, but that we continue to get it wrong. And we have the assurance, indeed, the reassurance, that through repentance and turning anew the benefits of living out in faith what Jesus has done in his dying and rising can be ours, forever.

Classically the story of human beings getting things wrong is given in the Genesis narrative of Adam and Eve. These two characters are types, they stand for you and for me, every one of us without exception. Whenever we get things wrong, omit to do that which we should do, or do that which we ought not to do, we fail God and one another. Our frailty and incompleteness is pictured in the Adam and Eve story.

---

8 My observations on this are based more on an imaginative and figurative interpretation of what is at play here rather than a strictly given expository analysis. Throughout the whole of this chapter, indeed throughout the book in fact, I have been very conscious that I write as a male and as a product of my own past and personality. The little autobiography I gave of myself in the Introduction is perhaps very pertinent in this regard.

What is interesting is that the Adam and Eve story is set in a Garden, the Garden of Eden. It is pictured as a perfect place until corrupted by human failure, disobedience and inadequacy. The garden, our world, remained in this state until Jesus came to put right that which was wrong. He is 'The Gardener' who by word and deed, by life, death, rising and ascending, has put right the wrong done in and to the garden by Adam and Eve, in other words by you and me.

To look at the world there remains much that is wrong. From the Christian perspective, the life of obedience and service to which Jesus calls us will bring in that new garden where 'The Gardener's' will is made real. It is perhaps no accident that the role of the gardener at the time of Jesus was a lowly servant role. Not unlike that role which Jesus took on when he washed his disciples' feet on that first Maundy Thursday.

In this sense perhaps we can say that, far from being mistaken, Mary of Magdala did indeed see 'The Gardener'.

Mary of Magdala is given her task and commission

In verse two above, we noted that Mary of Magdala had taken news of Jesus' absence from the tomb to Simon Peter and to the beloved disciple. Jesus now instructs her to say to them and to the others that he is to ascend, return, to the Father. This heralds his final departure from their visible presence. Henceforth his presence with them and with his church will be through the Holy Spirit, coming to live in their lives and in the lives of all those ready and prepared to receive God's Holy Spirit into their own lives.

Now in verse eighteen we find Mary of Magdala, in spite of the restricted legitimacy of one woman's testimony, nonetheless proclaiming to Jesus' brothers and disciples the outflow of faith that had by then taken hold of her, namely that she, ". . . had seen the Lord".

Simply to believe is not enough. To have faith means one has to live out the consequences of that faith, both in responsible tending and serving His Garden and those we meet within it, as well as drawing others into that same responsibility. Such is not easy in the secularised climate of western Europe. But the commission that the risen Jesus gave Mary of Magdala was meant for us as well as for those with whom she first shared it.

Bibliography

Amy-Jill Levine, *A Feminist Companion to John* (two volumes), Sheffield Academic Press, Sheffield 2002

Dante Alighieri, *The Divine Comedy: The Inferno,* translated and edited Robin Kirkpatrick, Penguin Classics, London 2012

Karl Barth, *Church Dogmatics:* vol. 4: Part One and Part Two, eds. G.W. Bromiley and T.F. Torrance, T&T Clark, Edinburgh 1958

Richard Bauckham and Trevor Hart, with illustrations by Helen Firth, *At The Cross; Meditations on People who were There,* Darton, Longman and Todd, London 1999

Colin Brown, General Editor, *The New International Dictionary of New Testament Theology,* (four volumes), The Paternoster Press, Carlisle 1986

Christopher Bryan, *The Resurrection of the Messiah,* Oxford University Press, New York 2011

Richard A. Burridge, *Four Gospels, One Jesus? A Symbolic Reading,* SPCK, London 2005

Richard A. Burridge, *John: The People's Bible Commentary,* BRF, Abingdon 2008

Richard A. Burridge, *What are the Gospels? A Comparison with Graeco-Roman Biography,* Cambridge University Press, Cambridge 1992

Ruth B. Edwards, *Discovering John: Content, Interpretation, Reception,* SPCK, London rev. 2014

Robert A. Gillies, *Three Days in Holy Week,* Handsel Press, Edinburgh 2015

Craig S. Keener, *The Gospel of John: A Commentary* (two volumes), Hendrickson, Peabody, Massachusetts 2003

Alan E. Lewis, *Between Cross and Resurrection: A Theology for Holy Saturday,* Eerdmans, Grand Rapids, Michigan 2003

Charles H. Talbert, *Reading John,* SPCK, London 1992

The New International Dictionary of New Testament Theology (four volumes), The Paternoster Press, Carlisle rev. 1986

The Calendar and Lectionary, General Synod of the Scottish Episcopal Church, Edinburgh 1996

The Harper Collins Study Bible, New Revised Standard Version, Harper Collins, New York 1993